The Complete Guide to Woodworking

The Complete Guide to Woodworking

Chris Simpson

NEW
BURLINGTON
BOOKS

ISBN 1-56138-409-7

Library of Congress Cataloging-in-Publication
Number: 93-87400

This book was designed and produced by
Quarto Publishing Inc.
The Old Brewery, 6 Blundell Street
London N7 9BH

Senior Editor Kate Kirby
Copy Editor Pamela Hopkinson
Senior Art Editor Mark Stevens
Designers Steve McCurdy, Tony Paine
Illustrators Rob Shone, Kuo Kang Chen
Plans David Kemp
Photographer Paul Forrester
Picture Manager Giulia Hetherington
Picture Researcher Susannah Jayes
Editorial Director Sophie Collins
Art Director Moira Clinch

Typeset in Great Britain by
West End Studios, Eastbourne
Manufactured by
Eray Scan Pte Ltd, Singapore
Printed by
Star Standard Industries (Pte) Ltd, Singapore

**With special thanks to Ian Styles of
Axminster Power Tools in Devon**

This book may be ordered by mail from the
publisher. Please include $2.50 for postage
and handling. *But try your bookstore first!*

Running Press Book Publishers
125 South Twenty-second Street
Philadelphia, Pennsylvania 19103-4399

Contents

3 Intermediate Course

4 Advanced Course

How to Use This Book

Furnituremaking is mainly learned by doing it. All the teachers and books in the world can only provide information. Learning comes through doing. This book starts from the premise that anyone can learn the skills necessary to make beautiful and functional furniture. The book is in the form of a carefully structured course arranged in four parts, including a Foundation course, followed by Elementary, Intermediate, and Advanced sections.

ABOUT THIS BOOK

This is not the kind of book you read through and then put down. It is a kind of workbook, full of specific instructions and advice. Try to think of it, as you read it, as your teacher speaking to you. This is a teacher you can turn to again and again.

Foundation course

If you have never done any woodwork before, then start here. The first part of the book introduces you to materials and tools. You learn about different woods and their uses, and about the variety of manmade materials available today. Your first basic kit of hand tools is introduced, and you are shown how to use and care for your tools.

More experienced woodworkers will find this to be a valuable reference section as well.

Elementary course

This part of the course opens with background information on understanding working drawings and the principles of joining wood – basic information that will stand you in good stead through all your woodworking projects.

Technique sections introduce new skills that will be put to use in the modules. These are your practical lessons. Here you will learn, as if your teacher was standing beside you, how to perform the actions of measuring and marking, cutting, shaping, joining, and finishing, all in clear, detailed step-by-step illustrations.

This is where you start to make your first pieces of furniture, a small table and a wall-hung cabinet. You will be guided every step of the way as you work through each module. Exploded diagrams and working drawings are supplied for each piece of furniture. The core of each module is a series of step-by-step photographs showing each stage in the woodworking process.

Intermediate course

The information is extended now, to bring

INFORMATION FEATURES

Practical information
Special information features introduce you to tools and materials. You will probably return to these time and again, dipping back into them to refresh your memory and increase your understanding as you progress through the course.

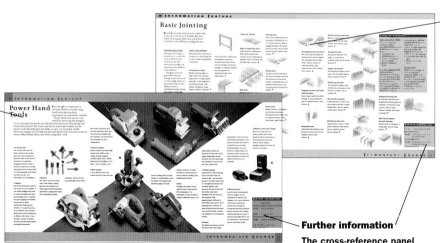

Theoretical information
These features outline the basic principles behind different aspects of woodworking. They clarify the reasons behind woodworking traditions: why certain joints work best in some situations and not in others, why furniture is made the way it is.

Further information
The cross-reference panel points you toward further information on the topic.

MODULES

Aims of the project
You will learn many things with each module; summarized here are the main techniques and skills.

Tools you will need
Tools listed in the order you will use them.

Time to allow
A rough estimate only; use this as a guide to help plan your work.

Remember
A reminder of some key points before you begin work.

Health and safety
So that you never forget you are working with potentially dangerous tools and equipment, you will be reminded of health and safety precautions before beginning each project.

Choosing wood
Suggestions for woods are provided to act as a guide when making your choice at your local lumberyard.

Plans
Working drawings supply a detailed "pattern." Measurements of each component mean you can cross-refer to the cutting lists.

Scale
The scale allows you to relate the diagrams to the full-size piece of furniture taking shape in your own workshop.

Exploded diagrams
The piece of furniture "taken apart" so you can see clearly how the joints are made and how every part relates to the whole.

Details
Selected details of the joints and construction techniques are further explained.

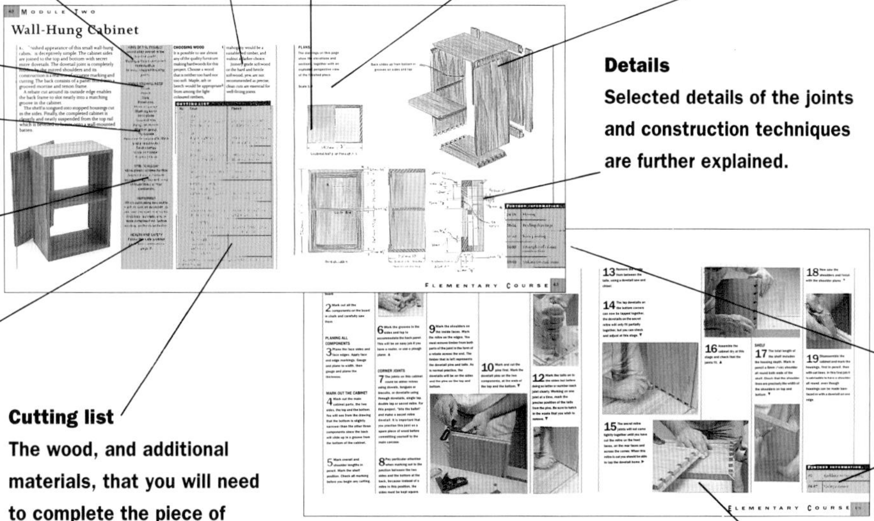

Further information
The cross-reference panel points you toward further information on the topic.

Cutting list
The wood, and additional materials, that you will need to complete the piece of furniture.

Step-by-step sequences
The author demonstrates each action for you, in color photographs with clear and concise captions, almost as if you were working side by side.

CUTTING LIST

No	Sawn	Planed
2	SIDES 2ft x 11in x 1in	1ft 10in x 10in x ¾in
1	TOP 1ft 5in x 11in x 1in 25mm	1ft 3in x 10in x ¾in
1	BOTTOM 1ft 5in x 10in x 1in	1ft 3in x 9¾in x ¾in
1	SHELF 1ft 3in x 10in x ¾in	1ft 2in x 9in x ½in
2	FOR FRAMED BACK STILES (UPRIGHTS) 2ft x 1¾in x 1in	1ft 10¼in x 1½in x ¾in
2	RAILS 1ft 4in x 2½in x 1in	1ft 2in x 2in x ⅞in
1	WALL BATTEN 12in x 1¾in x ½in	11in x 1⅝in x ⅜in
1	BACK PANEL manmade board approx. 1ft 7in x 12in x ¼in	

+ masking tape, finishing, adhesive, 2 screws for cabinet back, wall fixings for batten

Sawn measurements
The sawn measurements tell you what you need to buy from the lumberyard.

Planed measurements
You must reduce the wood to these measurements by planing before you begin the work of cutting and shaping.

Number of pieces
This tells you clearly the number of pieces to be cut in each size.

in power tools and man-made materials and the different skills needed to work with them. As you progress, you will continue to build on skills acquired earlier. Now you are introduced to more complicated constructions involving drawers, and to chair making.

The best of modern power and machine techniques are introduced alongside classic traditional hand skills.

Advanced course

You should be a skilled woodworker by now, ready to tackle complicated carcass constructions and hone your skills on fine woodworking projects. Advanced techniques of veneering, shaping, bending, and laminating are introduced here, with the opportunity to put each into practice on the final modules – two fine boxes and an easy chair. If you have worked through all the modules in order, these should present no difficulty – you will be guided through in the same carefully thought-out and detailed way.

TECHNIQUES FEATURES

Step-by-step sequences
Each new technique is introduced with a full demonstration, clear illustrations, and captions. These are the actions you will practice over and over again and that will form the foundation of your woodworking skills.

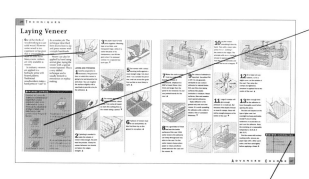

Boxed features
Whenever extra detail or additional information is needed, you will find an occasional boxed feature. They aim to help you understand more about the technique you are learning, or to perform it more efficiently and with greater understanding of the options available.

Further information
The cross-reference panel points you toward further information on the topic.

DESIGN FEATURES

Introduction
An introduction to the main features and developments in design of each piece of furniture covered in the modules.

Professional examples
Variations on each piece of furniture are to inspire you, and to demonstrate the different approaches of professional designers.

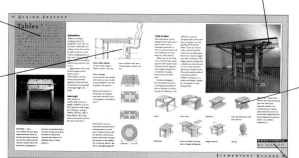

Design variations
Each piece of furniture can be varied in so many ways, and these illustrations aim to inspire you and widen your knowledge of design variations.

Principles of ergonomics
Illustrations show how the human body relates to furniture; these are the vital measurements and points on safety, comfort, and ease of use that all furnituremakers must consider.

Further information
The cross-reference panel points you toward further information on the topic.

SAFETY

Take sensible precautions and your workshop should be kept free from accidents. When dangers are recognized, they can be avoided. Knowledge means good working practice, as ignorance can lead to injury. Much of safe practice is common sense and thinking ahead. It is also important to develop the correct attitude toward tools – a balance of respect and caution.

Hand Tools
- Working practices have evolved so that cuts are made away from the body. Remember this and do not take risks.
- Keep tools sharp.

Power Tools
- Keep hands clear of moving blades and cutters.
- Read instructions thoroughly.
- Spend time looking at how the tool is made and works, with the power off.

Machinery
Realize what practices are potentially dangerous and avoid them by planning the job carefully.

- Always use push sticks.
- Always use the guards provided with the machinery.
- Remember that work can be caught by the saw or blade and thrown back at you.

Protection
- Whenever your eyes may be in danger, protect them by wearing safety glasses, goggles or a face mask.
- Wear ear protectors in noisy environments.
- Safeguard your lungs by wearing a mask or respirator.
- Use dust extraction on machinery.
- Ventilate effectively when finishing.
- Some adhesives and finishes can hurt the skin, so use gloves or barrier cream where necessary.

The Workshop
- Neatness is important.
- Keep the space where you work clear of material.

- Do not smoke.
- Dispose of dust and waste regularly to prevent fire.
- Install a smoke alarm.
- Keep a fire extinguisher in a prominent place.
- Keep a small first aid box for minor cuts and scratches.
- Include a pair of tweezers to remove splinters.

Goggles

Earmuffs

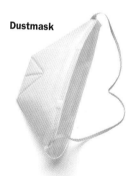

Dustmask

All-in-one respirator/visor

1 Foundation Course

All manner of people are drawn to the pleasures of woodwork, men and women, old and young, following many different trades and professions. What draws us all to this craft? Wood is good to use; it is clean, warm, and natural; and our efforts result in pleasing and useful pieces. We use a material provided by nature which is ecologically sound. Wood lasts, and wooden furniture often becomes an heirloom to hand down to future generations. Working with good tools is a pleasing and challenging part of the activity, and the mastery of skills gives a sense of achievement. This section introduces you to woods and materials and gives details of tools and how to use them – it covers the basic background information that you will need to know before starting. Enjoy learning and doing – and enjoy the results.

The Nature of Wood

Wood is a natural material; its very character and feel are a spur encouraging woodworkers to take up the craft. It is essential to have understanding of wood for effective and enjoyable working.

TREE GROWTH

The tree is a living organism that gives mankind great help – from oxygenating the planet to the provision of shelter and products. Water is drawn in through the roots and carbon dioxide taken in by the leaves, which then emit oxygen. Food is transmitted throughout the system.

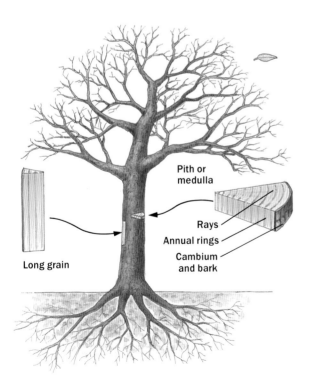

Long grain

Pith or medulla

Rays
Annual rings
Cambium and bark

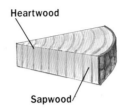

Heartwood

Sapwood

Heartwood and sapwood

The wood near the center of the trunk, the heartwood, carries little food; it is the structural support of the tree. The outer area transmits food and is called the sapwood. In some species, only the heartwood is used for woodwork since the sapwood is weak and prone to fungal and insect attack, while in others there is little difference, other than color, between the two. ▲

Annual growth

The tree grows by adding to its circumference each year, as well as to its height and breadth. At the center of the trunk is the pith or medulla — the remains of the sapling from which the tree grew. Then follows a series of annual rings, each depicting the growth cycle, normally of one year. Horizontal rays radiate from the center. On the outside, the cambium layer forms new wood, and bast and the bark ensure annual growth . ◄

SOFTWOODS AND HARDWOODS

These terms often cause confusion since they refer to the botanical characteristics of the tree. Some "hardwoods" are very soft – balsa wood, for instance – while some "softwoods" can be quite hard – yew is botanically a softwood.

Softwoods

Softwoods come from coniferous trees with needles instead of leaves which tend to remain during winter. Softwoods are composed of tracheids, short cells where food and moisture are transmitted between the sides of adjacent cell walls. Softwoods may have vessels or pores, but these are generally channels for resin. ▼

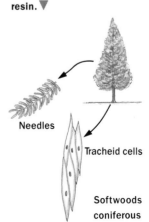

Needles

Tracheid cells

Softwoods coniferous

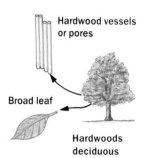

Hardwood vessels or pores

Broad leaf

Hardwoods deciduous

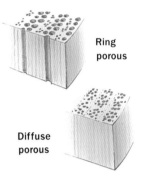

Ring porous

Diffuse porous

Hardwoods

Hardwoods come from deciduous trees; their leaves are shed in temperate climates each winter. The tree structure is made from long tubular vessels or pores which allow the tree to conduct moisture and food vertically. The horizontal rays carry food in a radial direction. Hardwood can be either ring porous or diffuse porous. Ring porous trees show clear annual rings marking the seasons, while diffuse porous trees live in areas where growth is year round. ▲

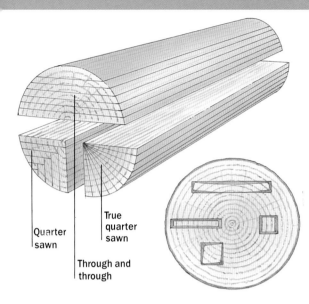

Quarter sawn

True quarter sawn

Through and through

Cutting

Wood is extracted from the forest as logs, mainly the trunk. Branch wood cannot usually be used, since its structure has stresses and strains present. The log is sawn into boards. Several different arrangements of cut are used. The most common

is where the trunk is simply cut in a series of boards. However, the board cut at the top tends to bow as it dries, and the annual rings try to straighten. Wood cut radially is very stable; therefore, logs are often cut radially or quarter sawn. ▲

SEASONING

Sawn boards still have moisture in the pores and cells, which must be removed before the wood can be used. The wood is therefore dried or seasoned and the moisture content reduced to an acceptable level. For wood used outdoors, moisture content of approximately 16 percent is suitable. However, if it is to be used indoors, it must be further

reduced, down to 8 percent, or even less in some cases.

Air drying is the traditional method of seasoning. The cut log is stickered outdoors with some form of cover over it. As a general rule, it takes one year for every 1 inch of thickness of the sawn boards. This method will not reduce moisture to less than approximately 16 percent and for interior

work the boards have to be mechanically dried.

The modern method of drying is by putting the wood in kilns. The stickered boards are placed on trolleys and put into the kiln, a large oven in which the temperature and humidity are precisely controlled. The kiln cycle starts with high humidity which is carefully changed to ensure that the wood is dried at the correct rate. Wood can be damaged if the wrong kiln schedule is used.

A recently developed

Re-stacking the boards

When the boards have been cut, it is necessary to re-stack them in the order they were cut, with spacers between each board to allow air to circulate. These spacers, called stickers, are always placed horizontally above one another. ▲

method, for small, valuable pieces of exotic wood, often used by wood turners, is to soak the wood in PEG (Polyethelene Glycol) which chemically converts the moisture.

FAULTS IN WOOD

Some woods have a natural resistance to fungal and insect attack (i.e. teak), but others need treatment by preservatives to give the wood some resistance. Generally, do not use wood in damp conditions where it may be attacked.

Faults may be found due to bad felling, poor seasoning, or erratic grain which causes trouble when wood is sawn. Wood may have shakes, checking, splits, be bowed or be twisted. When the board still has bark on it, it is called waney edged: it is advisable often with some woods to remove the bark and sapwood since these attract insects – often in softwoods. Dead knots can be a problem as they will fall out, and such wood should not be used in structural situations. In certain woods live knots add to the unusual feature of the wood.

PROPERTIES OF WOOD

Grain in some woods is straight and even, but you will find crossgrain which crosses in spirals around the tree, or interlocked grain when the spirals go different ways. Cross and interlocked grains are difficult to saw, plane, and finish – thus the saying "against the grain" – but it can result in attractive unusual features. Working "with the grain" is referred to frequently in the book.

Figure is when the grain runs in different directions, where the difference between early and late growth is marked, where color is present, where there are unusual features such as curl or burl – these all contribute to interesting figure in wood.

Texture in wood can range from fine, when the cells are small, to an open or coarse texture when the cells are large.

FURTHER INFORMATION	
134-135	Veneers

TYPES OF WOOD

There are many different species of wood, and their distribution throughout the world means that you will find certain woods in your locality that will serve your purposes well. The following short selection of woods is common in furnituremaking areas.

Common softwoods

Generally softwoods are used in building and joinery, but good-quality softwoods should not be considered as being inferior to hardwoods. They have their own uses. The nomenclature is confusing, however, since their common names do not always indicate their true botanical classification.

SCOTS PINE (*Pinus* species) also known as European Redwood.
Reasonable to work and has a very interesting figure. Its color matures with age and it is one of the most attractive of the softwoods.

DOUGLAS FIR (*Pseudotsuga* species)
Used for building work.

SITKA SPRUCE (*Picea* species)
Straight grain and even texture. Good to work, with a wide range of uses from boatbuilding to gliders.

CEDAR OF LEBANON (*Cedrus* species)
Good to work, but main attraction is its aroma, which is said to deter moths, so is often made into drawers.

YEW (*Taxus* species)
Tough and hard. Difficult to work but the most beautiful of softwoods. Very good for fine furniture.

Common hardwoods

The following selection is arranged without any consideration of locality, since color will direct choice.

OAK (*Quercus* species)
Coarse textured and straight grained, with distinct rays in the quarter sawn.

ASH (*Fraxinus* species)
Tough, straight grained, and supple; a good wood for bending, with an attractive finish. Generally white, but with dark stained heartwood.

MAPLE (*Acer* species)
Fine texture, hard, and straight grained. Popular for furniture and flooring.

BEECH (*Fagus* species)
Straight grained, even textured, reasonable to work, good for steam bending. Often used in furniture, particularly chairs.

SYCAMORE (*Platanus* species USA, *Acer* species, Europe)
Fine texture, generally straight grained (except for fiddleback grain used in musical instruments). Light in color, good in taking stain.

CHERRY (*Prunus* species USA)
Hard, fine textured, and straight grained; attractive coloring, good for furniture.

MAHOGANY (*Swietenia* species)
Medium texture, good to work, but many species. Varies from light color and weight, easy to work, to species which are darker, heavier, and hard.

WALNUT (*Juglans* species)
Good to work, the better boards have lovely color and grain. A lovely wood for all fine work.

TEAK (*Tectona* species) Substitutes – Iroko (*Chlorophora* species) and Afrormosia (*Pericopsis* species)
Coarse texture but oily feel. Good to work but hard on tools, requiring constant sharpening. Often used in the 1950s and 60s Scandinavian furniture with a simple oil finish.

ROSEWOOD (*Dalbergia* species)
Hard and heavy. Medium to work, but now very expensive and used for small fine work, inlay, and veneer.

EBONY (*Diospyros* species)
Very hard and dense, difficult to work, and one of the woods nearest to the color black.

PADAUK (*Pterocarpus*)
Hard, heavy, and fair to work. When cut, the shavings, sawdust, and surface are bright red, but on exposure to light, the wood quickly turns dark brown.

Specialist woods
Some woods have become prized for specific uses.

BOXWOOD (*Buxus* species)
Fine textured, dense, and heavy. Used for quality tool handles.

JELUTONG (*Dyera* species)
Soft and easy to work, a very good wood for pattern making and carving.

LIGNUM VITAE (*Guaiacum* species)
Very hard and heavy. Close interlocked grain. Difficult to work. One of the heaviest and most resistant woods. Used for mallets and wood pulleys and bearings.

MANUFACTURED BOARDS

Manufactured boards have been made possible by developments in adhesive and resin technology. These boards are generally inert, so that wood movement is no longer a problem.

Plywood: Odd numbers of veneers are glued with the grain of each sheet set at right angles to its neighbor. Plywood is normally available in 4 x 8 foot sheets, often with a decorative face veneer on one or both sides, which saves you from having to veneer large surfaces. Plywood is made using different grades of glue—interior grade uses urea-formaldehyde glues, while marine ply uses phenolic or Resourcinol-based adhesives.

3-Ply: Commonly used for drawer bottoms and cabinet backs; thicknesses can vary from 1/8 inch to 1/4 inch. Where the center veneer is thicker than the face veneers, this is called stout heart.

Multiply: Available in a choice of different thicknesses, used to construct furniture.

Birch plywood: Use for superior performance and quality, especially when making preforms. It looks good on its own with the surfaces finished.

Lumbar core plywood: These are similar to veneer-core plywood, except that the inner core is made of strips of wood. The width of the strips is usually about 1 inch.

Particle board: Wood is reduced to fibers and then glued back into sheets with synthetic resins. Particle board is used in the furniture industry and is available in several qualities.

Fiberboard: The edges of fiberboards need treating, generally by applying a solid or veneer edge banding. Medium Density Fiberboard (MDF) has been developed for furniture, since its edge can be surfaced (by hand or machine), and it will take finish directly.

Basic Hand Tools

The tools in this section provide a basic kit to start the projects in this book. Woodworking tools are precision instruments, and their purchase, storage, and use all need care if they are to last.

TOOL PURCHASE

Always buy the best tools you can afford. It is false economy to buy cheap ones. Price can be a guide but, more important, look closely at the tools and you will see the different qualities.

Buy tools made by a reputable manufacturer, but at this stage, do not be tempted to buy very expensive specialized handmade tools or antique tools; these are for the experienced woodworker.

Tool storage

Even a basic tool kit is a substantial investment, and to keep your tools in the best condition, consider how you will store them.

A traditional woodworker's tool chest has a hinged top and a series of trays, with a large open well in the bottom.

Unless you have such a chest handed down, this is not the best type of modern tool storage, since it is easy to lose tools at the bottom of the well.

The author's tool chest is like a cabinet with a door. The inside is fitted with drawers, shallow ones at the top, deeper at the bottom. This way, you can group tools according to their tasks.

There can also be problems with this design, since long tools will not fit unless you have a very large cabinet.

The very best way, if you have a secure, dry workshop, is to hang tools on wall-mounted boards. Each tool has its own place and can be "shadowed" with a paint outline so you can see if one is missing.

Methods of storage
It is not always easy to keep tools at hand in a traditional woodworker's tool chest. ▲

A series of drawers means tools can be grouped according to task. ▲

Hang tools so that each has its own marked place. ▲

Workbench

A woodworking bench is one of the first things you will need.

The bench must be sturdily made, and heavy enough not to vibrate as you plane or saw. It is often useful to attach it to the floor or a wall.

The bench vice is an essential part of the bench. You will need one of the following types.

The integral vice has wood jaws tightened by rotating a screw. It is often supplied mounted on the front of the bench with another mounted on the end.

The metal vice is larger, and you need one of a good size, with minimum 9-inch jaws with an opening width of up to 12 inches, preferably with a quick-release handle. You must fit hardwood vice "cheeks" to protect the work. ▲

1 Steel straightedge

Beveled and about 36 inches long x 2¼ inches wide x $^3/_{16}$ inch thick, a straightedge is useful for marking with a craft knife and for checking straight edges.

2 Steel rulers

These must have very clear markings for accuracy. A short one of 6 inches, another at 12 inches and a longer one at 24 inches are useful.

Retractable steel tapes

These are popular and necessary for measuring anything over 36 inches. They are unsuitable for fine work, but useful for marking wood before precise marking.

3 Try square

A try square is useful for marking right angles. Some are made for marking at 45 degrees, as well as at 90 degrees.

Steel combination square

With a cast metal fence which moves along the ruler and locks in position, this is an alternative to a try square.

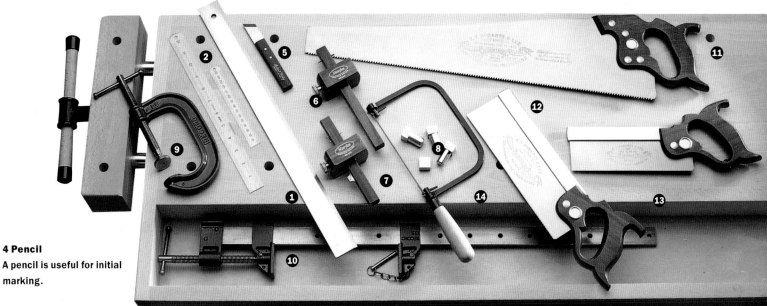

4 Pencil
A pencil is useful for initial marking.

5 Craft knife
Use a craft knife for fine work and where you are marking prior to cutting or chiseling.

6 Marking gauge
The marking gauge has a fence sliding along a beam, with a steel pin at one end which makes parallel marks. The fence is locked in place by a turn-screw.

Panel gauge
A panel gauge is similar to a marking gauge, with a longer beam and larger fence. It is used for marking wider boards.

7 Mortise gauge
A mortise gauge has two steel pins, one of which is adjustable to match the mortise chisel. The fence is also adjustable. It is used to mark mortises and tenons.

8 Metal bench dogs
These fit into holes drilled in the bench top to give a stop against which to work. Use them also with the end vice to hold or clamp.

9 C-clamps
In a variety of sizes, these clamps are very useful to hold work or for assembly.

10 Bar clamps
Bar clamps are mainly an assembly tool, but they can be used for holding.

11 Ripsaws
Ripsaws are for ripping along the grain, crosscut saws for cutting across the grain. Ripsaw teeth are sharpened to act like chisels, while crosscut teeth are sharpened like small knives to sever the fibers.

Your initial purchase, however, should be a panel (or dual-purpose) saw that can be used for cutting both along and across the grain.

Backsaws
Backsaws have a strip of steel or brass along the back of the blade for stiffening. You will need two kinds.

12 Tenon saw
A tenon saw, from 12 to 14 inches long, is useful for all general purpose accurate crosscutting.

13 Dovetail saw
Typically 8 to 10 inches long, the dovetail saw is used for fine work as well as dovetails.

14 Coping saw
A coping saw is used for cutting curves. The fine-toothed blade is held in tension in a frame. The blade can be swiveled so that you can cut in any direction up to the depth of the throat.

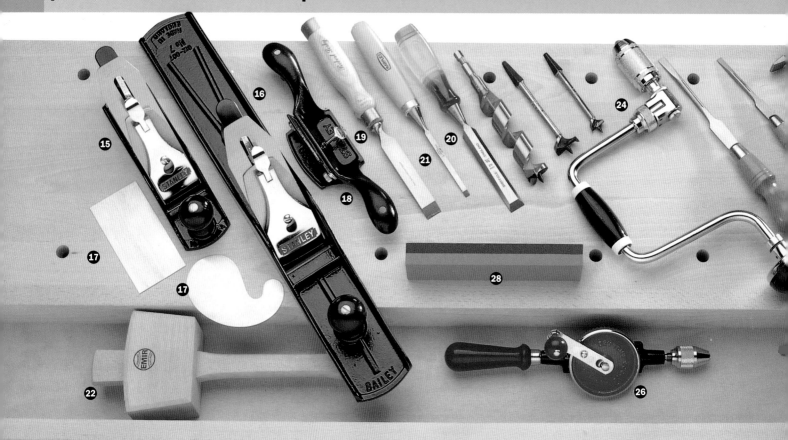

Bench planes

Bench planes smooth wood, reducing it to required width or thickness; they true up boards, square off ends, and smooth joints and surfaces before finishing. There are three main types.

15 Smoothing plane

This provides a smooth surface before finishing. However, since it is only up to 10 inches long, it often will not give a long, flat surface.

Jack plane or fore plane

The jack plane or fore plane, between 14 and 18 inches long, is a good general purpose plane which can be used for rough smoothing, joining, or final smoothing.

16 Jointer or trying plane

This is 20 to 24 inches long. It is ideal for truing up boards, planing long edges straight, and for general leveling.

You will need several different sizes of plane. Buy a jack plane first, then a smoothing plane and finally a trying plane.

17 Hand scraper

This is a piece of tempered steel, generally measuring 4 by 2½ inches and $1/16$ inch thick. The two long edges are sharpened to produce a burr of metal which removes very fine shavings. Scrapers can also be curved for scraping curved surfaces.

18 Cabinet scraper

The cabinet scraper is a steel holder that ensures the scraper blade is held in the right position and at the right angle.

19 Firmer chisels

Firmer chisels have blades that are rectangular in section for general work.

20 Bevel-edged chisels

These are less rigid since the sides of the blade are beveled to give clearance for working in corners or where there are undercuts.

Start with a small selection of bevel-edged chisels in sizes ¼, ½ and ¾ inch, then buy other sizes as you need them.

21 Mortise chisels

Mortise chisels are strong and heavy to withstand being hit with a mallet. They are used for cutting out deep recesses or mortises. They range in size from ¼ to ½ inch.

22 Mallet

The mallet is not only used for cutting mortises, but is very useful for tapping joints together.

23 Pin hammer

A pin hammer for tapping in brads or veneer pins will be most useful for furniture projects in this book.

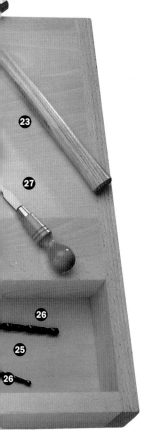

useful in small sizes, but for ¼ inch or larger holes, buy twist drill bits with brad points which are easier to use in wood.

27 Screwdrivers
These are necessary in a range of sizes; you will need at least three or four to start with.

28 Oilstone
An oilstone for keeping tools sharp is essential. When you are beginning, buy a stone with two faces – one with medium grit, the other with fine grit. Use light oil to lubricate the stone.

24 Brace and bits
For large work, you will generally use the brace which takes a range of bits. Anger bits are the most common. You will need a range of sizes: ¼, ⁵⁄₁₆, ³⁄₈, ½, and ¾ inch.

25 Countersink bits
Countersink bits for braces are also available. The auger bit is useful for drilling long and deep holes.

26 A hand drill with twist drill bits
This is better for fine work. Engineers' twist drill bits are

---

Use sandpaper to prepare wood for finishing or to shape wood, particularly to round edges. Sandpapers are graded by the coarseness of the grit: 600 is the finest and 50 is the coarsest. Sandpaper may be used by hand or in power sanders. For a perfect finish, work from coarse to fine grit, although planed or scraped surfaces may need only fine sandpaper. For perfect finishes, rub surfaces with fine sandpaper between coats of wax, paint, lacquer, or varnish.

TYPES OF SANDPAPER
Flint paper: This is used on softwoods and paintwork; it is not used for fine woodwork.

Garnet paper: Cuts cleanly leaving a smooth surface. It is available in very fine grit for hand or power sanding.

Aluminum oxide paper: Tends to be harder than garnet and often used with power tools. It lasts longer, but does not give as fine a finish.

Silicon carbide paper: This is used by metalworkers as "wet and dry" paper, but furnituremakers use a self-lubricating type, used dry, which is ideal for rubbing a polished finish.

Its hard grit makes it ideal for manmade boards, which can be difficult to sand because of their high glue content.

Steel wool: In its fine grades is used for smoothing between coats of finish or for applying wax.

grade	grit		applications
very coarse	50	1	heavy shaping
	60	1/2	
coarse	80	0	shaping – belt, disc, orbital, and hand
	100	2/0	
medium	120	3/0	shaping and finishing – belt, disc, orbital, and hand sanding
	150	4/0	
	180	5/0	
fine	220	6/0	finishing – power and hand sanding
	240	7/0	
	280	8/0	
very fine	320	9/0	final finishing, taking off sharp edges, sanding in between coats of lacquer – hand sanding
	360		
	400		
	500		
	600		

FURTHER INFORMATION	
9	Safety first
20-23	Tool maintenance
50-53	Advanced hand tools
76-77	Power hand tools

Tool Maintenance

All woodworking tools need regular maintenance. Every tool with a cutting edge eventually becomes dull with use, and dull tools are unsafe as well as hard to use. New chisels and planes also need honing to a razor-sharp cutting edge before they are used for the first time.

Keep all tools clean, try to have a place in the workshop to store each one where it won't get knocked or damaged, and wipe metal blades and parts with a light coating of oil to prevent rust.

Good tools are expensive, and even a basic tool kit represents a substantial financial investment, yet sharp and properly maintained tools are a joy to use and will last a lifetime.

GRINDING AND SHARPENING

Plane blades, chisels, and cutting gauges need to be ground and then sharpened on a stone.

● There are two main types of grinder, one of which is fluid lubricated. It is not advisable to use dry grinding wheels, as it is very easy to overheat the tool by over-zealous grinding, ruining the temper of the steel and the tool itself. If you have to use such a wheel, cool the tip of the tool *very* frequently in water. The use of fluid-cooled grinding machines, called motorized whetstones or wet/dry grinders, is preferable. Some good small ones are available for the home workshop with either a horizontal stone disk or a vertical wheel, lubricated with water.

● Use a sharpening stone for sharpening and honing. There are several different types, but when starting out you will probably use a synthetic stone made from aluminum oxide or silicon carbide and lubricate it with light machine oil. You will need several grits of oilstone, and it is possible to buy a combination stone. Choose one with medium and fine grits. As you progress with woodworking, you may like to consider some of the alternatives to synthetic stones. Natural Arkansas stones are excellent oilstones. Japanese water stones have a wide range of hardness grades, while diamond-sharpening stones are also available.

● Where the lubricating medium is oil, it is necessary to keep the surface clean. After much use, the stone will become clogged and need cleaning with kerosene. A waterstone needs to be immersed in water to saturate it, and it must be kept wet during use.

● For final honing after using an oilstone, use a leather strop with stropping paste, fine carborundum powder, or jeweler's rouge to produce a razor-sharp edge.

● If your stone becomes hollow after repeated sharpening, it can be flattened by grinding on a sheet of plate glass with carborundum powder as a cutting agent.

MAINTAINING AND ADJUSTING PLANES

A modern metal plane is a precision tool and requires precise adjustment every time the blade is removed for sharpening. Even once it is set up, the blade can be knocked out of true by a jolt or by dropping on the bench.

Protect the plane blade by retracting it each time you store the plane. Store it on its side on a shelf, or in its box.

Wipe it occasionally with an oily cloth to prevent rust.

If you have difficulty planing smoothly, check the metal casting to see that the sole is perfectly flat. On a quality tool, this should be the case, but if it is not, you can flatten the bottom of the plane by applying some carborundum powder to a sheet of glass and rubbing the plane over it. This is a lengthy process, but should result in a finely tuned tool.

SHARPENING PLANES

Some woods dull plane blades very quickly, and with difficult woods you may need to sharpen a plane blade every ten minutes or so; but even with the best wood, you will still need to stop and sharpen the blade more often than you might at first expect.

Plane blades are normally sharpened at two angles. The ground angle is at 25 degrees, which you should not need to touch for some time; the sharpening angle of 30 degrees will probably have to be honed before you start work and requires regular sharpening.

A plane blade needs a razor-sharp edge, and to get the sharpest blade possible, use an oilstone followed by a leather strop with some very fine carborundum powder or jeweler's rouge. You should be able to see and feel the sharpness of the blade at this stage. However, in feeling the edge, be careful not to cut yourself.

When you first buy a new plane, it is worth taking it carefully apart so that you are familiar with its components and how they work.
It is useful to tune or humanize a new tool by giving some attention to smoothing the handles and removing any sharp edges on top of the plane that might make its use uncomfortable.

Anatomy of a plane

1   Lever cap
2   Locking lever
3   Cap iron
4   Blade
5   Cap iron locking screw
6   Frog
7   Lever cap screw

8   Lateral adjustment lever
9   Depth adjustment lever
10 Depth adjustment knob
11 Sole
12 Rear handle
13 Front knob
14 Mouth

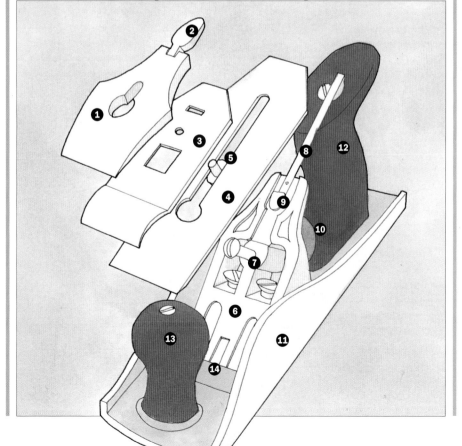

Dismantling and sharpening a plane blade

1 To remove the blade, lift the lever; this releases pressure on the blade and allows removal of the lever cap. ▶

2 Lift the blade and cap iron out of its seating, and holding the blade and cap iron assembly, loosen the screw holding the two together, and remove the cap iron. ▶

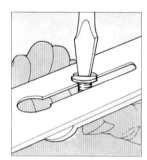

3 To sharpen the blade, rub the angled side on an oilstone. The other side must be left perfectly flat. Hold the blade firmly, keeping the angle, about 30 degrees. Work the blade back and forth along the oilstone. ▶

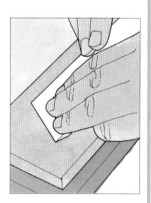

FURTHER INFORMATION	
9	Safety first

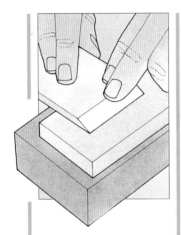

Replacing the blade and adjusting the plane

1 Fit the cap iron back onto the blade. To avoid spoiling the sharp edge, rotate the cap iron in position behind the front edge and carefully move it forward to within about ¹/₃₂ inch of the edge. The nearer the cap iron is set to the blade, the finer the cut. ▼

4 A burr or sliver of metal will now have appeared on the other (flat side) of the blade. Carefully remove this by laying this face of the blade flat on the oilstone, and taking a few strokes. Repeat the process of honing and removing the burr. For a razor-sharp final edge, use a leather strop. ▲

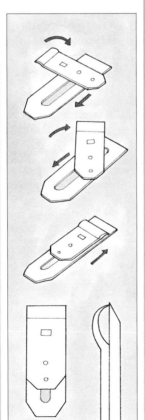

2 Make sure the cap iron and blade fit tightly together to prevent shavings from wedging between them. Carefully set the blade and cap iron back into the plane and lock in place using the lever cap. ▶

3 Hold the plane at eye level and sight along the sole to see the projecting blade. Use the lateral adjustment lever to make sure the blade projects parallel with the sole across its width. Move the lever from side to side. ▶

4 Depth of cut increases as the blade is pushed out by turning the depth adjustment nut. The cutting edge should appear as a fine black line. For fine work the blade should hardly be visible. ▶

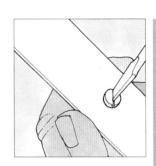

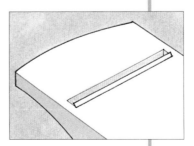

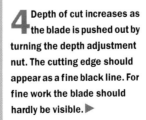

MAINTAINING AND SHARPENING CHISELS

Like a plane blade, a chisel has a ground angle and a sharpening angle. The manufacturer supplies the chisel already ground to an angle of 25 degrees; you will not generally have to work on this angle, but the cutting edge of the chisel must be honed to between 30 degrees and 35 degrees and kept razor sharp by regular honing on an oilstone.

Protect chisels when not in use by storing them carefully, either in a wall-mounted rack, if you have the space, or by keeping them rolled up in a cloth.

Sharpening a chisel blade

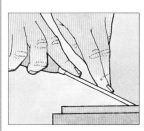

1 Hold the blade at the correct angle and move it with a forward and backward motion along the oilstone. Put pressure on as you move forward, release it as you move backward. ▲

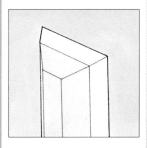

2 Be sure to keep the edge being produced square with the edge of the chisel blade. After a few strokes, check to see that the bevel is forming evenly and test carefully with your thumb to feel if the burr is forming on the back. ▲

3 Remove the burr by stroking the back of the chisel flat on the sharpening stone. Repeat the process of honing and de-burring as with the plane blade, and finish off on a leather strop. ▼

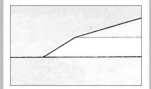

4 When sharpening narrow blades, it is important that you do not wear a groove in the oilstone. Move blades around in a figure-eight pattern to utilize the whole surface of the stone, being careful not to dig the edges of the blade into the stone. Very narrow blades may be sharpened on the edge of the stone. ▼

MAINTAINING SAWS

A sharp saw needs no forcing through the wood, but a dull saw cuts slowly and will wander from the cutting line, and may jam or buckle if forced. The saw is one tool which is difficult for an amateur to sharpen. Good "saw sharpeners" need a lot of time and experience to perfect their skills, and many woodworkers prefer to send their saws to a saw sharpener rather than to do it themselves.

Many modern saws are available with hard-tipped blades which last much longer than traditional blades, but which cannot be re-sharpened.

Coping saw blades are disposable and should be replaced as soon as they become dull.

Whether you use traditional or modern hard-tipped blades, you can prolong the life of all your saw blades by keeping them clean, wiping the blades with an oily cloth occasionally and protecting them from damage when not in use.

The teeth can be protected by sliding a plastic sleeve over them, and if possible, hang each saw up on the workshop wall.

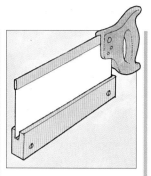

2 Handsaws can be supported at their blade end with a wooden "bridge" over the blade, while backsaws can have their teeth resting in a groove in a piece of wood. This also protects the blade. ▲

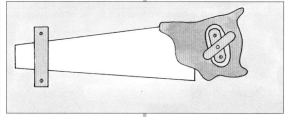

Hanging saws

1 The best way of hanging saws is to make a shaped block that fits into the hand-hold in the saw handle, with a rotating toggle to hold the saw in place. ▲

Planing

Planing prepares the wood for the accurate marking and cutting out of joints, and smooths the wood ready for the finishing steps. The plane blade must be razor sharp and carefully adjusted to take shavings of the depth required. Planing is a skill that takes practice to acquire – be prepared to spend quite a lot of time getting used to the tool, and to learning the techniques needed to sharpen, adjust, and use it accurately.

Planing sequence

There is a sequence to planing that should be followed at nearly all times. Plane the face side, then the face edge. Then gauge and plane to width, and finally plane to thickness. Sawing a component exactly to length is left until later.

Choice of plane

A long plane gives a more accurate result. It rides over high spots on the wood, gradually removing them until the wood is even and a single long shaving can be taken off. A smaller plane follows the contours of the surface. A smoothing plane or small jack plane makes a good choice for a first buy.

Set the plane to take a fine cut at first until you are used to the action. There is less resistance and more control than if you set the blade to take a thicker cut. As you plane, adjust the blade until you are taking a good shaving from the surface.

HOW TO PLANE

1 Begin by choosing the better side of the board, which will become the face side. Hold the board on a firm horizontal surface, against a bench stop, or in a vice for small pieces. Stand with shoulder, hip, and plane in line for full control, feet slightly apart. ▼ ▶

2 Aim to work with a smooth motion, applying even pressure. As you pass the plane over the wood at the beginning of the stroke, pressure is on the front handle. ▶

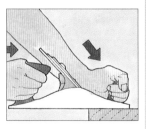

3 In mid-stroke, press evenly, and as you reach the end of the stroke, transfer pressure to the rear handle. Don't lift the plane up until the plane blade is beyond the end of the board. ▶

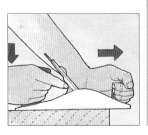

Squaring the wood: Planing face side, face edge, width and thickness
Think of planing and checking for straightness and squareness as one skill, one is of little use without the other. Stop frequently to check the wood. Always lay the plane on its side when you put it down, to prevent the blade being damaged.

4 As you plane the face, stop and check the wood carefully for flatness across the width; and sight along the wood to check it for straightness. ▲

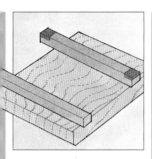

5 To check for "winding" or twisting, place two wooden strips at each end and sight across the tops to see if they are parallel. ▲

6 Place a steel ruler or straightedge along the grain at intervals to check that the surface is flat along its whole length. Alternately, tilt the plane on its side and use that as a straightedge. ▲

Planing the edge

7 To plane the face edge, put the wood against a bench stop or in a vice. To keep the plane centered on a narrow edge, put your thumb on top of the sole near the handle and run your fingers along under the side to guide the plane. ▼

8 Use a square to check that the edge is square with the face along its whole length. Be sure to push the stock of the square tight up against the face side of the wood. Hold the wood up to the light if possible. ▼

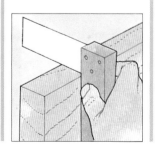

Marking and planing the other sides

9 Once you have a face and edge that are perfectly straight and at right angles to one another, mark them with the face and edge mark. With these surfaces true, it is relatively easy to make the wood the width and thickness you need for your project. ▶

10 Use a marking gauge to mark the width of the board from the face edge. Set the gauge to the width, hold the fence against the face edge, and gauge a line.
  Turn the board over to mark the width on the sawn, unplaned side. Again, run the fence of the gauge against the face edge. Plane, or saw and plane, the board to this width, checking frequently. ▶

11 To mark the thickness required, run the fence of the marking gauge against the face side, marking a line on the face edge and one on the far edge. Then plane the board down to these marks. Stop and check the work often for squareness. ▶

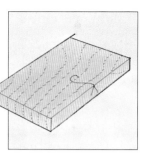

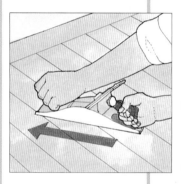

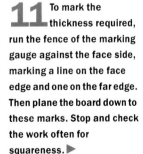

Planing wide boards

Plane wide boards, or boards that have been joined together, working diagonally, with and across the grain in overlapping strokes to cover the whole surface. Finish by taking fine shavings in parallel strokes in the direction of the grain. ▼

FURTHER INFORMATION	
9	Safety first
16-19	Basic hand tools
20-23	Tool maintenance
130-131	Power planing

Chiseling

The action of chiseling is called paring. Depending on the task, you will either be paring vertically, or paring horizontally. Sometimes you will be working to cut away a complete end or face; at other times, particularly to make joints or to cut mortises, say for hinges, you only need to chisel part-way through the wood.

Always work to a marked line and work within the waste area first, carefully paring wood away up to the marked line. Remove only small amounts of wood at a time. As a general rule, cut the wood across the grain first, make any cuts along the grain afterward, to avoid splitting the wood.

A narrower chisel gives you more control as it has less resistance from the wood.

Secure the wood firmly, and if you are going to cut right through it, place a piece of scrap wood beneath it to protect the workbench.

Holding the chisel

Always hold the chisel in such a way that you cannot cut yourself, keeping hands behind the cutting edge at all times. Use one hand to guide the chisel blade, while the other hand holds the chisel and supplies the force required.

PARING VERTICALLY

Hold the chisel bevel outward. One hand guides the blade to remove small amounts of wood each time, working up to the cutting line. With the other hand, apply the pressure from the shoulders.

When working across the grain, sever the fibers with a series of parallel cuts to loosen them before making the final cut to the line. ▲

PARING HORIZONTALLY

1 Hold the chisel bevel upward. The thumb on the blade acts to guide the chisel, while the other hand applies the pressure. ▶

2 For additional power, lean into the work, applying body pressure from the waist. ▶

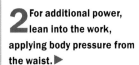

USING A MALLET

Chisels are hit only with mallets, never hammers. Normally, a chisel should be sharp enough to do its work without being hit by a mallet, although most modern chisels are tough enough to withstand tapping with the mallet. Generally, you only hit a mortise chisel, or a firmer chisel, when removing waste from mortises. ▶

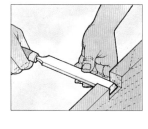

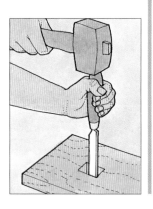

Sawing

Accurate sawing takes a lot of practice, but it calls for precision on your part, not force. The aim is to let the saw do the work. A good saw should feel well-balanced and cut smoothly almost under its own weight. Your task is to guide the saw, not to press it down.

The steps shown here refer to cutting across the grain, and cutting right through a piece of wood. When you are cutting joints, you will be using the same technique to cut along the grain or only part-way through the wood.

SAWING PRACTICE

1 Holding a square against the face side and face edge, mark pencil lines across the wood on the face side and down the face edge. ▲

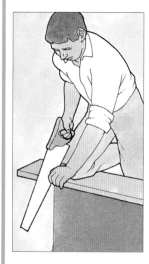

2 Hold the wood firmly and stand so that the blade is in line with your arm and shoulder. Start the cut with a few strokes on the far corner, guiding the blade against your raised thumb. ▲

3 After the first few strokes, you should have the beginnings of a saw cut. Now start taking longer, steady strokes. Watch the pencil line across the face side and direct the cutting edge of the saw to the waste side of that line. ▼

4 Saw steadily, and keep checking that your cut is remaining on the line, both across the face and then as it starts to go down the edge. ▼

PRECISION SAWING

1 Now you are used to the action, practice more precise sawing. Using a knife, mark a cut line on all four surfaces. Start the saw cut on the face side at the far edge, as in step 2 left. ▶

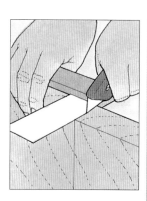

2 Saw on the waste side of the marked line, watching continually that you do not wander from it. Saw carefully with the saw at a high angle, then lower the saw to begin cutting across the face side. ▶

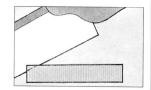

3 Once you have made a kerf on the face side for the saw to run in, start cutting down the face edge. You will see that you have now cut a triangle as defined by these two faces. ▶

4 Sawing the third surface is relatively easy because the cuts already made will guide the saw, and you should be able to concentrate on watching the line and checking that the blade is not deviating from the cut that you have made. ▶

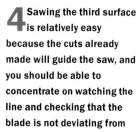

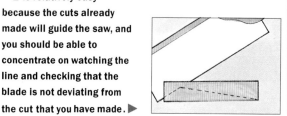

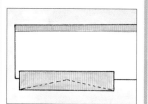

5 As you complete the cut, carefully make the final few strokes. Support the end of the wood with your hand so that the cutoff does not fall and splinter the board. ▲

FURTHER INFORMATION	
9	Safety first
16-19	Basic hand tools
20-23	Tool maintenance

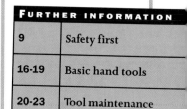

It is exciting to see a piece of furniture take shape. In this chapter, the first two modules introduce basic frame and carcass structures. The small table is an ideal project to introduce mortise and tenon joints, and the cabinet gives you your first experience of making dovetails. Both projects are fairly simple, but will give you the chance to master preparation, marking, joining, assembly, and finishing. This experience, once mastered, provides the basis for the other projects. At this stage, take it steady. Do not worry about mistakes; just gain the basic skills that will bring much reward later.

Reading Drawings

All but the simplest projects require an accurate scale drawing to be completed before making any piece of furniture. The drawing allows you to check proportions, measurements, and construction details. There are basic drawing conventions followed by designers of all kinds, including furniture designers. These conventions, once you understand them, speed up the drawing process and remove any possibility of misunderstanding between designer and maker.

As an example, Module 2, the wall-hung cabinet, is used here to demonstrate various drawing techniques and conventions.

SKETCH DRAWINGS AND 3D PROJECTIONS

Nearly all designers will begin with rough sketches, working them up to progressively more detailed and accurate drawings. Even if you have no drawing skills, you can still follow the same process using the drawing conventions and the basic projections.

Projections allow a 3-dimensional object to be represented on a flat piece of paper. This exploded 3D view of the wall-hung cabinet is a sophisticated illustration of an isometric projection, but it still keeps to certain basic conventions which anyone can follow with the help of a T-square and a 30/60 degree try square. All vertical lines are drawn vertically, and all other lines are drawn at 30 degrees to the horizontal.

Exploded diagrams
Exploding the components allows hidden details to be clearly seen. The exploded drawing can be used to begin to work out proportions.

Details of joint construction can be accurately worked out.

For accurate working, this joint detail will need to be drawn up as a full-size plan later.

SCALE DRAWINGS

Most drawings need to be reproduced to scale if they are to be a manageable size. The scale chosen should suit the size of the object being drawn and will always be indicated on the drawing.

Again, there are conventions in the choice of scale which most designers will follow. For individual pieces of furniture, a scale of 1:4 is common. This means that on the drawing ¼ inch equals 1 inch or 3 inches equals 1 foot on the piece of furniture.

For larger pieces of furniture or room layouts, a scale of 1:24 is common.

Small items or details may be drawn full-size or even larger, and joints, moldings, and other details are often drawn alongside scale drawings of the whole piece of furniture. It is quite common for drawings to include several items at different scales.

In recording dimensions, the convention is to write all measurements between extension lines for clarity. All dimensions should be placed so that they are readable from the bottom right-hand corner of the

Types of projection
A first-angle projection imagines the object suspended in a square corner and being projected back onto the three surfaces. ▼

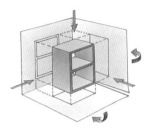

In a first-angle projection, the corner is cut along the red line, and opened out flat to produce the drawing. ▼

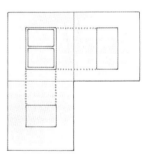

drawing.

Dimensions should be complete enough for full cutting lists to be worked out from them.

The first-angle projection and the third-angle projection are commonly used for accurate scale drawings. Both make use of the front view (front elevation),

A third-angle projection imagines each face of the object projected forward onto a glass corner. ▼

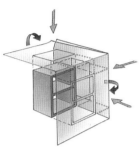

The glass corner is cut and opened out flat to produce the drawing. ▼

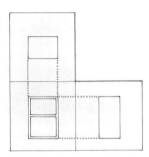

placing side views on the left or right, and a plan view at the top or bottom.

Third-angle projection
The third-angle projection is one method of laying out a drawing. ▶

"Grain" lines are an accepted convention to represent sections through solid wood.

B-B, indicated here, relates to the further internal details that are included on the plan view.

Enlarged details
An enlarged detail clarifies the way in which the back components fit together and the way the cabinet attaches to the wall bracket. ▶

Broken lines indicate where the full-size drawing has been "compressed" to exclude parts that do not require this detailed treatment.

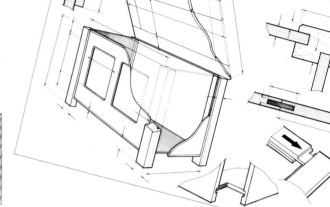

Here, the plan view includes a sectional half plan taken through B-B (below).

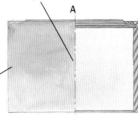

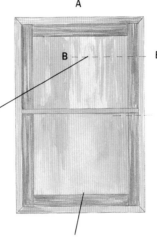

The front elevation allows accurate internal and external dimensions to be shown.

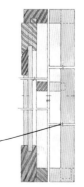

Sectional views are slices through the work to show internal construction details. This sectional side elevation has been taken through the center line or A-A.

Other types of plan
You will encounter other types of drawings in books and woodworking magazines.

A popular convention is to use a scaled-down grid over a drawing, such as the one used in Module 8 the easy chair. This is particularly useful when components require curves and shaping. Draw a full-size grid and plot where the lines of the drawing intersect with the grid.

A 3-dimensional cutaway drawing with detail annotations is another way of showing how intricate or shaped components fit together. ▲

FURTHER INFORMATION	
62-67	Module 2: wall-hung cabinet

Basic Joining

Generally woodworkers have to deal with material in the form of boards. Because wood has a grain direction, joints have evolved to suit different configurations.

JOINING AND GLUING

With glue technology as advanced as it is, why have joints at all? Joints have evolved so that their mechanical strength is as important as the addition of any glue.

End grain cannot be glued effectively; any attempt to join end-to-end or end-to-edge results in a poor bond. A face-to-face glue bond is reasonably strong. Joining long edge to long edge gives a very good bond, as does joining an edge to a face.

Good joining aims for mechanical strength and the best gluing situation where as much wood as possible is jointed face to face. A simple bridle joint for example, has poor gluing between shoulders and the face, but good gluing between the face and the joint.

JOINT DEVELOPMENT

Most joints have evolved as a variation on a peg fitting into a hole to make a mechanical connection.

Principles of joints

Boards meeting edge-to-edge call for two possible approaches: a simple glued edge-to-edge joint, or the addition of mechanical means, with tongue and groove, loose splines, dowels, or biscuits. ▼

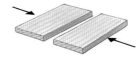

A flat wood frame can use miters, lap joints, bridle joints, dowels, or mortise and tenons. In manmade board, you would try to cut from the whole board. ▼

A rail and stile or underframe arrangement would use mortise and tenons. These may be through, and may be wedged or blind. Joining this arrangement in manmade board is not appropriate. ▲

For a corner joint, use a dovetail. Or use a simple butt or miter joint reinforced with veneer splines, dowels, loose splines, or biscuits. ▲

To fit a partition, use either a dado or sliding dovetail. Manmade boards could use a dado but a tongue, biscuit, or butt joint may be sufficient. ▼

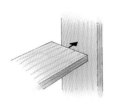

TYPES OF JOINTS

Edge-to-edge joint

Traditionally a rubbed joint. With modern glues and clamps can be simply glued together. Not very strong. Use for table tops; panels. ▲

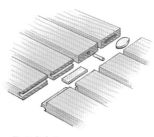

Butt joint

Mechanically strengthened with tongue and groove, loose spline in two grooves, dowels, or biscuits. The board faces come precisely together, reducing planing. Use for table tops; long panels. ▲

Miter joint

Needs reinforcing with dowels. Decorative keys or splines cut from wood or veneer can be glued in. Use for picture frames; framing a central panel. ▲

Lap joint

One of the simplest joints for two pieces meeting in an L or T or cross formation. May be pegged through with dowels. Not very strong. Use for small simple frames; cabinet door frames. ▼

Bridle joint

An open mortise and tenon — the tenon is usually one-third the thickness of the wood, except when connecting pieces of different thicknesses. Use for leg and rail connection on tables. ▼

Dowel joint

Widely used as a substitute for mortise and tenons. Strong and easy to make. Use for cabinet frames; doors; table tops; table frames. ▼

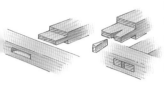

Through mortise and tenon
The tenon goes through the mortise and is often wedged. The strongest end to edge joints. Use for frames in cabinetmaking; table underframes; chair frames; door frames. ▲

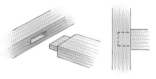

Blind mortise and tenon with shoulders
Used in good-quality furniture making. A strong rigid joint. Use for cabinet frames; chair frames. ▲

Sloping haunch
Used when the mortise is near the top of a leg or rail. Use for cabinet frames; table frames. ▲

Double mortise and tenon
Where a wide rail goes into a vertical stile. Use for table frames; chair frames; door frames. ▶

Through dovetail
Strong and attractive. The finger or box joint is machine-made. Use for boxes; drawers. ▶

Half-blind dovetail
The end grain is hidden on one piece. Use for joining drawer sides to drawer fronts. ▶

Full-blind dovetail
The dovetail is hidden. Only the thin line of end grain on the tail part is visible. Use for cabinets. ▶

Secret miter dovetail
A difficult joint to make. From the outside looks like a simple butted miter. Use for cabinet construction; drawers. ▶

Reinforced butt joint
Using screws or pins, or miter joints reinforced with dowels. Use for cabinet corners; picture frames. ▶

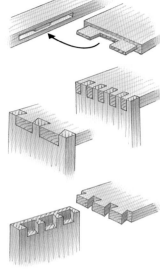

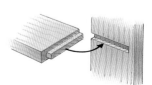

Blind dado joint
An effective and easy joint. Stopping the dado gives an unbroken vertical line on the carcass. Use for attaching shelves; holding rails inside carcasses. ▶

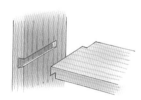

Sliding dovetail
Should need no clamping. A strong joint. Use for attaching shelves. ▼

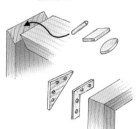

Small Table

The techniques and processes used in making this small table can be applied to many other designs which use a frame construction. The finished table is a classic, timeless design. Its construction covers many of the processes that will form the basis of further projects: wood selection and sawing, measuring and marking, cutting joints, making a mitered frame, and finishing.

In later projects and as your tool kit increases, you may consider using power hand tools or machinery. However, at this stage, "bite the bullet" and master these basic processes by hand. The feel of the hand tool is basic to an understanding of the material.

AIMS OF THE PROJECT
Provide a foundation in basic techniques and processes. Precision cutting and fitting of a number of identical joints.

TOOLS YOU WILL NEED
Chalk
Pencil
Ruler
Try square
Panel saw
Marking gauge
Craft knife
Jack plane
Tenon or dovetail saw
Mortise chisel
Bevel edge chisels
Mortise gauge
Rabbet plane or shoulder plane
Drill and drill bits
Nail set
4 bar clamps
Cabinet scraper
Sanding block

TIME TO ALLOW
If this is your first project, much time will be spent in learning basic processes and developing skills, so be prepared to spend what time is necessary to achieve the best possible result.

REMEMBER
Read through the instructions and plan the project in your mind.

HEALTH AND SAFETY
Follow the safe working procedures outlined on page 9.

CHOOSING WOOD

Your choice will be based on color, workability, availability, and cost. Hardwood is preferable to softwood when beginning furnituremaking. Softwoods are not recommended, since they do not saw or chisel crisply. For this first project, buy wood with a straight grain. You will not need to maximize grain pattern or avoid defects, so laying out will be simplified.

Color

Choose a wood that will relate to the place where the table will be used.

Lighter woods could be English oak, American white oak or beech, maple or sycamore. Medium woods could be mahogany, teak, or American red oak, and dark woods could be American black walnut, French walnut, or rosewood.

Workability

Choose a wood that works well, is not so soft that it is difficult to achieve crisp saw and chisel cuts, nor so hard that it is brittle. The wood should have a close grain and good working properties.

No	Sawn	Planed
4	LEGS 1ft 10in x 1½in x 1½in	1ft 7in x 1¼in x 1¼in
4	TOP RAILS 12in x 2in x 1in	9½in x 1¾in x ¾in
4	BOTTOM RAILS 12in x 1½in x 1in	9½in x 1¼in x ¾in
4	TOP FRAME SIDES 1ft 4in x 3¼in x 1in	1ft 2in x 3in x ¾in

+ masking tape, finishing, glue, dowels, screws and sheet material for inset top measuring 9 x 9 x ¼ inches

PLANS

The drawings on this page and overleaf show the elevations and sections, together with an exploded perspective view of the finished piece.

Scale 1:11

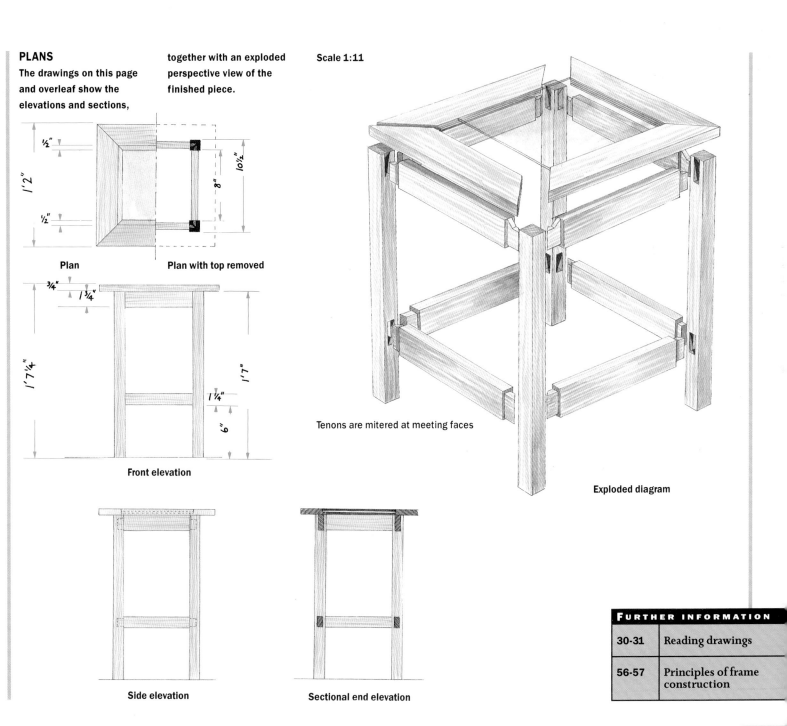

Plan

Plan with top removed

½"
1'2"
½"
8"
10½"

Front elevation

¾"
1¾"
1'7¼"
1¼"
1'7"
6"

Tenons are mitered at meeting faces

Exploded diagram

Side elevation

Sectional end elevation

BUYING WOOD

1 Buy wood in rough form. You must make an allowance for waste in converting it from its rough state to planed to size.

The length of 9½ inches for the rails allows 8 inches between shoulders plus ¾ inch each end for tenons. Two thicknesses of boards are needed 1½ and 1 inch. Buy one board of each thickness from which to cut the components.

MARK AND CUT COMPONENTS

2 Mark the components on to the sawn board with chalk, making an allowance for the saw cuts. ▼

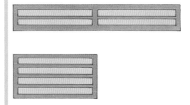

3 Cut the components from the marked board, using a hand saw.

4 Plane all components and mark them with face and edge marks.

LAY OUT LEGS OF TABLE UNDERFRAME

5 Mark the four legs together. Set the legs with the face sides uppermost and the face edges toward you. Hold them together with a clamp. ▲

6 Using a pencil, mark the length of the legs and the position where the rails will be attached. Then mark the length of the mortises.

The lower rails have a small ⅛ inch shoulder on the top and the bottom. The top rails have a shoulder on the bottom and a sloping haunch at the top. A haunch is a shortened portion of the tenon. It helps lock the joint to prevent the frame from twisting out of line.

7 Pencil in the mortise waste. Then at the top and bottom of the legs at the mortise positions, scribe a line with a craft knife ⅛ inch inside the pencil marks indicating the rail positions at the ends of the mortises.

TRANSFER MARKS TO THE FACE EDGE

8 Unclamp the four legs and, with a try square, transfer all the pencil marks from the face side to the face edge. Then transfer the scribe lines on the ends and at the ends of the mortises, and pencil in the waste. This will give you four legs, with joints marked on the eight inside faces. Complete the top and bottom cut lines all around the legs.

GAUGE MORTISES

9 Set the mortise gauge pins to the width of the mortise chisel at the pin points. Then set the gauge so that the mortise marks are central on the legs; do this by marking the points from one side, then turning and marking from the other side, adjusting to correct any discrepancy. Make the marks from the face side and edge.

10 Mark the eight rails of the table underframe, four top, and four bottom. Clamp the upper set together, and mark the lengths on the four face edges with a craft knife. Mark the length of 8 inches between the shoulders, plus an extra ¾ inch on each end for the tenons, giving a total length of 9½ inches. Take off the clamp. ▼

11 Now repeat this procedure with the lower set of rails clamped together. Use the scribe lines on one of the top rails to mark the precise position on this set, to make sure both are exactly the same.

12 Check the marking and transfer these lines to the other three faces of each rail. Always use the square from the face side or the face edge. ▲

13 Cut the rails exactly to length. Then, with the pins of the mortise gauge as already set to the mortise chisel, adjust the stock to center on the rails and mark the tenons around the end of the rails. Now mark the shoulders and haunches on the tenon sides, using a marking gauge. Pencil the waste that will be removed. Re-check all marking.

CUT MORTISES IN LEGS

14 There are 16 mortises to cut in the legs. Remember to cut to the shoulder line, not the penciled position of the rail. ▲

15 Hold the work in the vice and chop out the waste up to the lines.

16 In the eight mortises for the top rails, make the entry for the haunch and saw down at the ends of the mortise. ▼

17 Chop out the waste to accept the haunch. ▼

SAW TENONS ON RAILS

18 There are eight tenons with haunch and shoulder, and eight with two shoulders. Saw down to the shoulders on all tenon pieces in the same way. Then cut the sloping line of the haunch. ▶

FURTHER INFORMATION	
26	Chiseling
26-27	Sawing
44-46	Making a mortise and tenon joint

19 Lay each piece flat to cut the main tenon shoulder. ▼

DRILLING FOR THE SCREWS

20 Mark two drill holes in the underside of each top rail for the screws to hold the top frame. With a small table like this, it would be difficult to drill the top rails to accept screws after the frame is glued up.

21 Countersunk screws are needed when a deep rail is to have a top attached by screws. To simply drill a clearance hole for the screw, with the screw head at the bottom face of the rail, would require very long screws. Therefore, drill a hole larger than the screw head

only part way through the rail, from the underside. The screw then sits in a hole at a pre-determined depth, allowing a shorter screw to be used.

Mark carefully, drill the clearance hole for the screw, then countersink for the screw head to the required depth. ▼

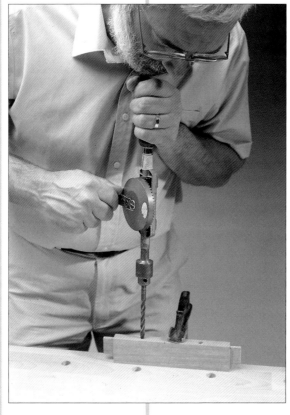

NUMBER AND FIT ALL JOINTS

22 Number or letter each joint and carefully fit each tenon into its mortise. With practice it will be possible to make the mortise and tenon so they fit accurately from the saw, but it is likely that for some time you will have to pare with a chisel to fit the joints. ▲

23 It is standard practice, as in this design, for the rails on all four sides to be at the same level. Therefore, the tenons at each corner will meet, and it is necessary to cut a miter on the end of each tenon so they fit in the mortise together. Check and re-check that you have marked this correctly before you cut.

FINISH INSIDE FACES

24 You will soon be ready to prepare for assembly, but with this design it is best to finish all the inside faces first. Scrape and sand the four faces of each rail and the two inside faces of each leg. Then mask all of the joint faces, so that the chosen finish will not prevent gluing and apply the finish.

CLAMP TWO SIDES

25 Remove the masking tape. Assemble the two side frames dry, without glue, and test that all joints fit tight. ▼

26 Check that the frame is square and flat. Check inside angles with a try square. ▼

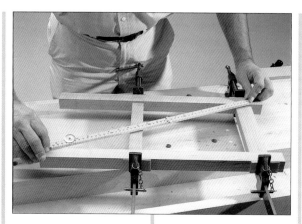

27 Measure the diagonals to check that they are identical. If all is well, apply glue and clamp with bar clamps, using small blocks of wood between the outside of the legs and the clamp faces to prevent damage. ▲

CHECKING FOR SQUARE

28 It is vital at this stage to check again to make sure that the frame is square and not twisted. If the frame is out of square, this can be remedied by adjusting the position of the clamps, but the dry assembly should have already shown any problems.

REMOVE EXCESS GLUE

29 When clamping is complete, remove the excess glue. Either do this when the glue is wet, using a damp cloth and water, or wait until the glue has cured to a gel and remove it with a chisel.

If you wait until the glue is hard, damage can be caused to the surfaces around the joints. Also check the mortises and clean out any glue that may prevent the final assembly.

ASSEMBLY OF THE WHOLE FRAME

30 Clamp the whole frame dry again, check that all joints fit, and that the structure is square in all directions. ▼

FURTHER INFORMATION	
70	Holding and clamping
60-61	Finishes

31 This process is slightly more complex than assembling the individual frames, but if you arrange the clamps as shown there should be no problems. ▲

32 If all is well dry, then disassemble, apply the glue, and clamp the frame. Remove excess glue. ▲

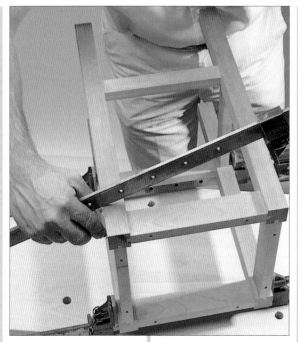

33 When the glue has cured, remove the clamps. Carefully saw off the waste at the top and bottom ends of the legs, and plane these end grain surfaces flat. ▲

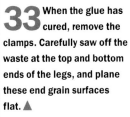

34 Scrape and sand the outside of the frame. ▲

35 Check all pre-finished surfaces and apply an overall coat of finish. ▲

LAY OUT THE TOP FRAME

36 The four pieces for the top frame have already been planed square. Mark the miters at the corners and saw accurately to this line. Glue triangular scraps to the corners to aid assembly. Then plane the miters so that all faces fit. You will need to place the frame together and carefully trim the miters to achieve a perfect fit. ▶

CUT THE RABBET TO HOLD THE CENTER INSERT

37 This can be done before or after the above process, but *must* be completed before the frame is assembled and glued. The rabbet is to be ¼ inch deep so that it can accept a veneered plywood insert, or a sheet of glass or mirror. In later work you will probably use hand power tools (a router) or machine tools to cut rabbets and grooves, but for this project it is worth using the hand tools, either a rabbet or a shoulder plane. ▶

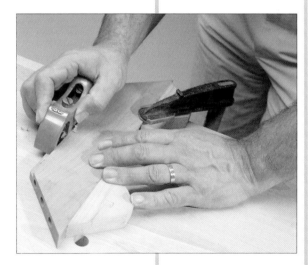

MARK THE DOWEL POSITIONS

38 The top frame could be assembled using tongues or biscuits. For this first piece, dowels are the safest method, since the joint cannot slip when it is being clamped up.

39 Gauge a center line along each miter face. Then carefully align the four frame pieces in the vice. Mark the centers of the dowel holes, making a scribe line across the four ends to intersect with the gauged center line on each piece. ▼

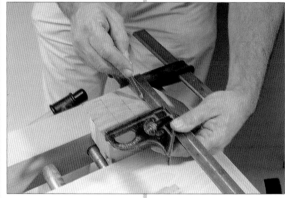

40 Mark location points for the dowel drilling using a nail set. ▼

FURTHER INFORMATION	
70	Holding and clamping
88	Biscuit joining
118-119	Dowel joints

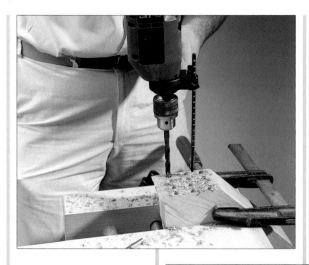

41 Drill the holes for the dowels. Make sure that the drill is held upright. ▲

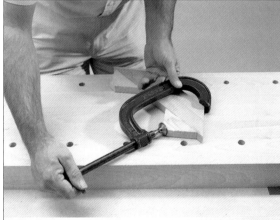

42 Cut the dowels to length. Fit them loose in the holes and clamp the joints dry. You may need to make final adjustments to the miter faces at this stage.

ASSEMBLY

43 It is possible to use four bar clamps to clamp this frame, and this method works with dowels better than with tongues or biscuits where the joint can slip out of place. A preferable method is to glue triangular scraps to the outside corners of the joints. ▲

44 When the whole frame is assembled, the blocks enable you to apply clamping pressure at right angles to the joint face. ▲

45 If the joint is tight when clamped dry, apply glue and finally clamp. ▼

46 When the glue has cured, remove the clamps and chisel or saw off the triangular blocks. ▶

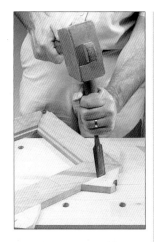

47 Plane all outside surfaces. ▼

48 Screw the underframe to the top frame. ▶

49 Scrape, sand, and finish the frame. ▶

TOP INSERT

50 If you choose glass or a mirror, give the glass cutter a precise cardboard template, since it is very difficult to fit glass that is even slightly oversize.

51 If you decide that you would like an insert with a wood finish, cut a piece of ¼ inch plywood, with veneer applied to one face. ▼

52 The finished table, a pleasing addition to any setting. ▲

FURTHER INFORMATION	
47	Preparing the surface
71	Finishing
146-147	Veneering

Making a Mortise and Tenon Joint

There are many different mortise and tenon joints, each suitable for a specific purpose. Along with the dovetail joint, the mortise and tenon is one of the most common joints found in woodwork. Practice making the joint before you begin work on a real project.

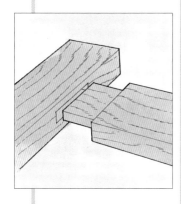

The standard stop mortise and tenon joint (shown above) is described on these pages. In the project sections, there will be examples of how this basic joint is adapted for specific purposes.

The wood

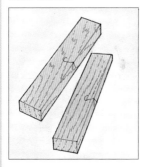

For this practice exercise, take two pieces of wood (which can be softwood, or an easily worked hardwood) each measuring approximately 10 inches long by 2 inches wide by ¾ inch thick (shown above).

Both pieces of wood must be finished smooth with flat surfaces and edges that are square. The ends should be square also.

Plane the first face straight and flat, plane the edge flat and square, mark these with the face and edge marks and finally plane to width and thickness then square both ends.

MARKING OUT THE JOINT

1 Set the mortise gauge precisely to the mortise chisel. However, do all the marking with a pencil first, and check your marking before you make the final cutting marks with the marking knife or mortise gauge. ▼

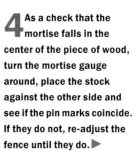

2 On the face edge of the piece of wood that is to contain the mortise, or hole, mark the width of the tenon piece, i.e. 2 inches, using a pencil and a square. Then as a guide, mark at right angles down the face side and the reverse side. This shows where the tenon will fit. ▼

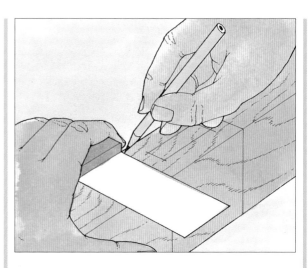

3 It is usually a good idea to make the tenon with shoulders all around, so put a further set of marks ⅛ inch inside the lines you marked first. ▲

4 As a check that the mortise falls in the center of the piece of wood, turn the mortise gauge around, place the stock against the other side and see if the pin marks coincide. If they do not, re-adjust the fence until they do. ▶

5 With a mortise gauge, hold the fence firmly against the face side, and mark the two parallel lines for the mortise in the center of the wood. ▶

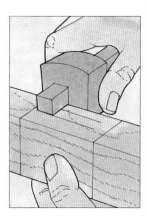

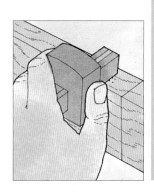

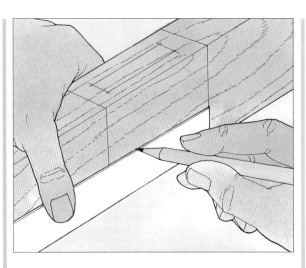

8 Take up the tenon piece. The length of the tenon will be equal to the depth of the mortise. Mark all around the tenon, 1½ inches from the end. Use the marking knife for this as you will be sawing from these marks. ▶

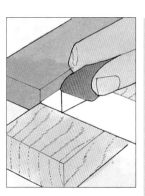

11 With the marking gauge set to ⅛ inch, mark the tenon edge shoulders. ▼

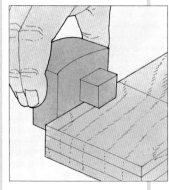

6 Mark the precise depth of the mortise in pencil on the face side. Make this mortise 1½ inches deep. ▲

7 With the knife, make two cut lines over the pencil marks on the face edge where the mortise will end. As a general rule, use the pencil for guidance marks and cut or gauged lines when you will saw or chisel to that line. ▶

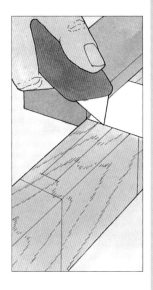

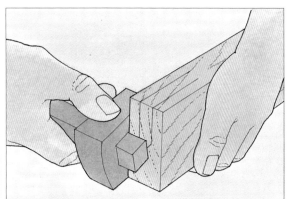

9 With the mortise gauge at the same setting, and with the fence held against the face side, first gauge around the face edge and the end. Hold the other end of the wood in the vice to do this. ▲

10 Turn the wood in the vice so that you can gauge the other edge, again with the fence of the mortise gauge held against the face side. ▶

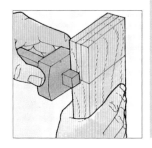

FURTHER INFORMATION	
9	Safety first
24-25	Planing
26	Chiseling
26-27	Sawing
34-43	Module 1: small table

CUTTING THE MORTISE

There are several ways to cut a mortise; the method given here is one of the simplest.

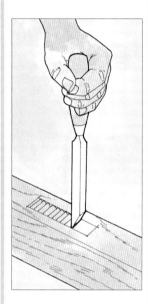

1 Hold the mortise piece securely on the bench, or in the vice, cushioned with scrap wood. Hold the chisel vertically, locating it within the guidelines and chop across the grain to a depth of ⅛ inch, every ⅛ inch or so. Do not chop right up to the end of the mortise for the moment. ▲

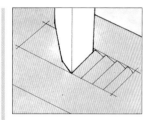

2 You should now find that the chopped bits of wood chisel out very easily from between the gauged lines.

Repeat this procedure, chopping down about ⅛ inch each time, until you have reached a depth of about 1½ inches. A piece of masking tape around the chisel blade, 1½ inches from the end, will help guide you. ▲

3 When you have reached the required depth, work up to the cut line to finish off the ends of the mortise. You should now have a mortise hole that is the required width for the tenon. ▲

CUTTING THE TENON

1 Hold the tenon piece in the vice, and with the tenon saw, saw down the gauged lines to the knife cut. Stop about ¹⁄₃₂ inch short of this knife-cut shoulder line. Remember to saw on the waste side of the wood. ▶

2 Saw at an angle of 45° down across the front of the tenon.

3 Then saw down across the back.

4 Saw down to the shoulder.

5 Turn the wood around and repeat the operation on the other ⅛ inch lines.

6 Hold the tenon piece against a support and saw down the shoulder on each of the four sides to a depth of no more than ⅛ inch. ▶

7 Put the wood back in the vice and saw down the two ⅛ inch edge shoulders. This reduces the tenon to the width of the mortise. ▶

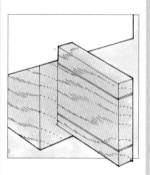

8 Finally, return to the other shoulder lines and saw the waste pieces off. Check very carefully that you do not go too far. You should now have a sawn tenon that fits into the chiseled mortise. ▼

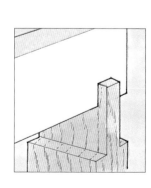

9 Fit the tenon into the mortise and clamp up the pieces; the shoulders of the tenon should fit precisely up to the face edge of the mortise piece. A skilled woodworker would fit the tenon straight from the saw, but in the early stages you will probably have to make some modifications with a chisel. ▼

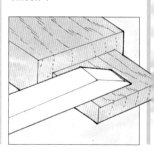

Preparing the Surface

Before finishing a project, the whole surface must be flat and smooth. It is sometimes possible for an expert to produce such a surface with a plane, but normally you will need to use other tools and techniques to achieve a smooth, even surface, particularly on woods which have interlocking grain or other surface difficulties.

HOW TO USE A SCRAPER

Using a scraper to finish hardwoods requires practice. The aim is to take a very thin shaving; if you start producing dust and not shavings, then the scraper is dull and needs re-sharpening. This process generates heat in the metal of the scraper – be warned, your thumbs can get quite sore.

1 Hold the scraper in both hands, thumbs toward you. Grip the scraper so that you are bending it into a slight curve away from you. If the corners of the scraper start to dig into the wood, increase the curve slightly. ▲

2 Start with the scraper vertical, then tilt it away from you until the burred edge is brought into contact with the wood. Push the scraper away from you to cut a thin shaving. ▲

HOW TO USE A SANDING BLOCK

Always go to the trouble to use a sanding block when sanding by hand. However hard you try, if you simply use the paper in your hand, you will cause your smoothly planed or scraped surface to develop irregularities, and this will show up when you apply the finish.

A cork sanding block is firm, but slightly resilient. It should be a convenient size to fit your hand.

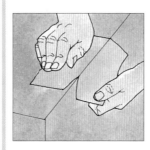

1 Standard-sized sheets of sandpaper can be torn into quarters to fit around a sanding block. Tear the paper over an edge, such as the work bench. ▲

2 Hold the paper tightly around the block, with the chamfers on top. ▶

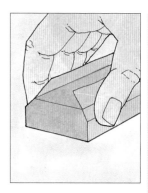

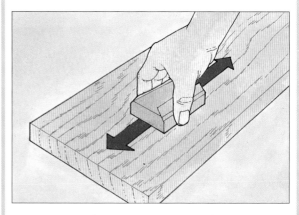

3 Always rub the paper along the grain and never across it. Sanding across the grain will create minute scratches on the surface which will be difficult to remove, and which will often show when you apply the finish. ▲

FURTHER INFORMATION	
9	Safety first
20-23	Tool maintenance
24-25	Planing
26	Chiseling
26-27	Sawing
34-43	Module 1: small table

Tables

The classic mortise and tenon underframe used for the Small Table in Module 1 can form the basis for many other designs. Using the same construction, but changing the size, you can make anything from coffee tables to family-size kitchen or dining tables.

A taller table becomes a pedestal for displaying plants or other objects.

The choice of wood and finishes also contributes to the design. Ash, maple, oak or beech are all suitable choices for a modern table of any size. The surface can also be stained or finished with paint or lacquer.

NIC PRYKE • Table
A very simple structure, given added dimension and lift by the inlay decoration on the top unit and the contrast with the extension and the sides. This decoration is appropriate to the piece and besides being a fine piece of inlay work, gives the table an interest and character that makes for an individual piece of visual quality. ▲

ERGONOMICS

Tables for eating or working need to be designed so that they can be used comfortably and without strain. You need to be able to pull up a chair without banging knees or feet, and to have enough elbow room to eat without obstructing someone next to you.

Ergonomics is the study of how human bodies relate to their environment, and this science has provided optimum measurements for furniture to suit people of average height and build.

Table height

Most adults are comfortably seated at a height of 1 foot 5 inches. The optimum table height for working or eating is 2 foot 4 inches, while at least 2 foot of leg room is necessary between the rail and the floor.

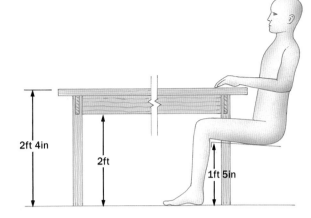

IDEAL TABLE HEIGHT
The ideal table height is 700mm (2ft 4in); ideal leg room is 610mm (2ft); ideal seating height is 430mm (1ft 5in).

Place settings
To eat in comfort, the average adult needs an area of table measuring 2 foot wide by 1 foot deep. ▶

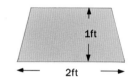

Whatever the shape of a dining table, the designer must allow sufficient space for the people it is intended to seat. ▶

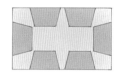

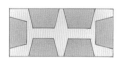

Round tables can be an especially economical way of seating people in a small space. A table of only 3 foot 3 inches diameter will seat four people comfortably. Increase the diameter to only 4 foot to seat six, and to 5 foot to seat eight people. ▶

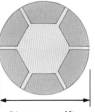

Diameter = 4ft

TYPES OF TABLE

The underframe can be designed with solid wood legs or panel ends in manmade materials, or with a central crossrail and two endframes as in the refectory table (below).

Table tops can be made with a miterd frame. Solid tops are traditionally made of boards joined together with tongue and grooves or dowels. Nowadays biscuit joints are often used.

Furniture designers have devoted much time to solving the problem of how to increase or reduce the size of a tabletop, to suit different occasions. Dropleaf tables need some form of support, as with gateleg and Pembroke tables. There are various styles of draw-leaf table, where the top slides apart. Extra leaves may be hinged upward, or slotted in. The hinge and pivot design has a double top, which pivots on one corner and then opens up to double its size. This top should be made of manmade board for stability. A tilting top is a traditional design, suitable for occasional or small dining tables.

NIC PRYKE • *Dining table*
The low view of the photograph gives the table great dramatic qualities. The contrast between wood, glass, and metal works very well, and the engineering and honest approach to structure make a very positive statement. ▲

Frame

Panel ends

Refectory

Gate-leg underframe with drop-leaf top.

Pembroke

Draw-leaf table with loose leaf or integral folding leaf.

Hinge and pivot

Tilt top

FURTHER INFORMATION

| 34-43 | Module 1: small table |

Advanced Hand Tools

As your skills develop and you undertake more complex projects, the basic tool kit will need to be supplemented.

If you decide to purchase power hand tools or machine tools, a few of the tools shown here will not be necessary, for example, the work of the rabbet plane and the router plane will be done by a power router; the bowsaw will be covered by the bandsaw; and the panel or keyhole saw will be covered by power jigsaw or fretsaw.

Other specialized tools will be necessary, and the best policy is to buy them as and when they are needed. In this way you will build up a very comprehensive collection.

1 Rabbet plane
The rabbet plane blade extends across the width of the sole. It can plane wide rabbets as well as narrow ones. It has no fence or guide, so rabbets must be started against a batten nailed or clamped to the work.

2 Block plane
A small, lightweight bench plane, the block plane is used one-handed for planing end grain, chamfers, and delicate work. Add extra pressure when required by placing your other hand over

the toe. The blade is set at a shallower angle than other bench planes and is fitted with the bevel upward.

3 Shoulder plane
The shoulder plane can be used like the rabbet plane, but is most useful when working long miters on secret miter dovetails, planing shoulders or other fine work.

4 Router plane
This smooths, cuts, and cleans up grooves and

recesses. It is useful before you proceed to a power router. It often saves time in setting up the power router.

Some of this tool's work can be accomplished with the router plane.

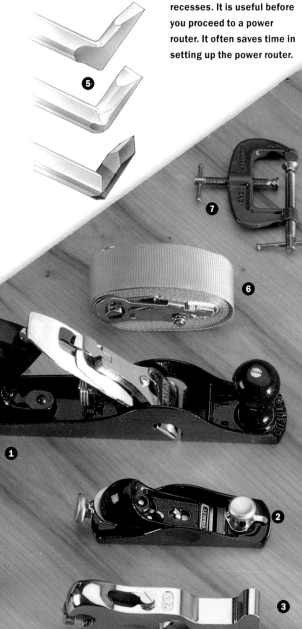

5 Router bits

The bits are set at a shallow angle and work with a paring action. The choice of bits available makes it a versatile tool.

6 Band or web clamps

The band or web clamp consists of a length of nylon webbing tensioned by a ratchet mechanism. It applies equal pressure on all corners and is useful where bar clamps are too heavy or awkward, for example, in gluing frames with mitered corners, particularly small picture frames, and often in chair making.

7 Edge clamp

The edge clamp is a small C-clamp with an extra screw and metal bar. It is used when applying edge bandings to a surface; the side pressure pad pushes the edge band tight. However, for this to be really useful, quite a number are needed.

8 Sliding bevel

This is invaluable for any angle other than 90 degrees or 45 degrees. It can mark or check both internal and external angles. Set the slotted blade against a protractor or the work. In some projects in this book, it is used to mark dovetails instead of a dovetail template.

9 Vernier caliper

A vernier caliper is useful for many measuring tasks. You do not need an expensive engineer's caliper; the small plastic variety with a dial is sufficient. As your work progresses, you will find you reach the level of accuracy required for this tool.

10 Bowsaw

The bowsaw cuts curves and is strong enough to cut quite thick wood. If you do not have power hand tools, a bowsaw is the only way of cutting large curved work. It is difficult to use and needs some practice and great care in cutting to the line.

11 Gents saw

The gents saw is extremely useful where a fine cutting line is needed, even though a dovetail saw is often suitable. The fine teeth leave a very smooth finish.

12 Keyhole saw

The keyhole saw was originally used to cut keyholes. A power jigsaw or fretsaw can do the job of cutting holes away from an edge, but there are often times when it is more useful to use this little saw. Drill a hole first in which to start the cut.

FURTHER INFORMATION	
9	Safety first
16-19	Basic hand tools
20-23	Tool maintenance

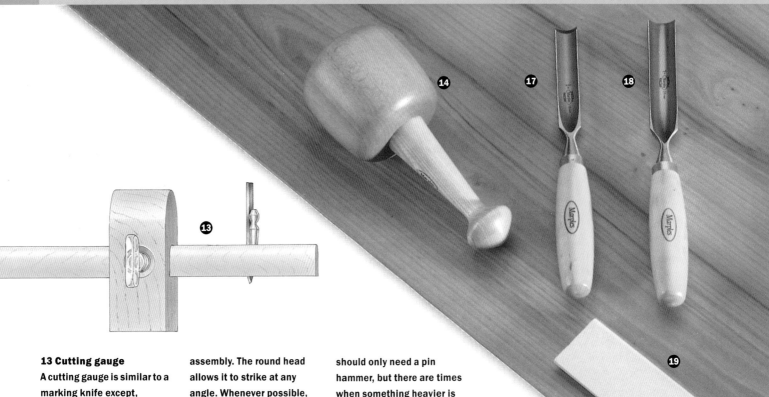

13 Cutting gauge

A cutting gauge is similar to a marking knife except, instead of a point, a blade is inserted in the end. Use it for marking across the grain, parallel to an edge. It is also useful for cutting veneer. The blade can be removed and sharpened.

14 Carver's mallet

This is a most useful tool both for making joints and for assembly. The round head allows it to strike at any angle. Whenever possible, use a piece of scrap wood between the furniture and the mallet to protect the surface.

15 Claw hammer

A good general-purpose tool where you need the weight of a heavier hammer, but with more direction than a mallet. Most furnituremaking should only need a pin hammer, but there are times when something heavier is needed. The claw is designed to extract nails.

16 Nail set

A nail set is used to drive nails below the surface of the wood. The point diameter should be slightly smaller than the nail head. A nail set can often be used with a pin hammer, but there may be occasions when you will need to use a claw hammer.

17 Firmer gouge

Used to make cuts which are not square, this gouge is sharpened on the outside of the curve with the cutting edge on the inside of the curve. This is used to scoop out hollows or grooves.

18 The scribing gouge

This is used for trimming curved shoulders.

19 Slip stone

A slip stone is necessary to sharpen the curved blades of gouges. Its curved profile enables you to work on the

23 Rasps

The rasp is a coarse file; it removes wood quickly and leaves a rough surface which is smoothed by a file. These too are used for shaping, particularly for chairmaking. A range of different types and sizes are illustrated. All are useful but a favorite for many jobs is the circular or rat-tail shape, both file and rasp.

24 Riffler files

Riffler files have shaped ends in many different configurations, and they are often the only tools which will allow you to cut into very awkward places in shaped work. You can buy them with rasp heads at one end and file heads at the other.

22 Spokeshaves

Spokeshaves are made to smooth either internal or external curves. External curves can often be cut with a plane or chisel, whereas internal curves can only be smoothed by the spokeshave. The blade is set by the two fine screws. A well-sharpened spokeshave can leave a finish on hardwoods that needs no sanding.

It will take time to get used to this tool so that you take clean cuts and the blade does not chatter or jump.

The craftsman of old would often make his own spokeshave, making the handle to fit a purchased blade. If you get the chance to buy a spokeshave blade, do so, and experiment with it. The homemade spokeshave is often superior to the metal tool.

20 The pump action or spiral ratchet screwdriver

This saves time and effort when a lot of screws have to be inserted. It works via straight pressure on the handle or can be closed and used like an ordinary screwdriver. When using the pump action, always hold the chuck to prevent it from slipping.

21 Chuck

Chucks come in a variety of sizes.

inside faces of a gouge. Most other sharpening can be done on a combination oilstone.

FURTHER INFORMATION	
9	Safety first
16-19	Basic hand tools
20-23	Tool maintenance

Workshop Planning

Wherever you begin woodworking, you will want to develop a workshop dedicated to the task of making furniture. You need to consider environmental factors such as heat, ventilation, and light, as well as the layout of the bench and machines, and access for material in and furniture out. A small workshop cannot have space dedicated to each activity; each space must be used for several tasks.

WORKSHOP PLANNING
Draw a scale plan of your workshop and make cardboard cutouts of the bench and machines. Mark the locations of doors, windows, and power outlets, and experiment to find the best situation for each item.

Manmade board and wood are heavy and take up a lot of space. You will also need to reach hardware easily.

Each machine needs space around it. Materials must be able to pass through saws and planers unobstructed, and on most other machines, the material projects to one side or another. When planning, make sure one machine does not interfere with another.

Incoming material
Wood can be up to 15 feet long, and manmade boards are typically 4 x 8 feet. Full-size sheets may have to be cut in the yard or by the supplier. These materials must be kept in the workshop so they remain dry with even temperature and humidity while they are being made up.

Storage
Finish, hardware, glue, and other supplies can be stored in well-planned shelves, drawers and cupboards. It is worth taking time in planning and making them.

If you do not hold large stocks, bring them into the workshop, but try to put them in a secure, possibly fireproof, cupboard.

Workbench
A sturdy bench is essential. Position it, if possible, in natural light, near a window; if not, good artificial light is necessary.

Hard floor surfaces get very uncomfortable if you are working for long periods. Lay industrial rubber matting around the work area in front of the bench.

Cutting and assembling
All the projects in this book are relatively small, but the desk and chair need more assembly space than you may think. Leave space for a couple of sawhorses so wood can be laid down for chalking and rough cutting, and for assembling cabinets. Consider height as well as ground area for large items like sideboards, dressers, and dining tables.

Finishing
Your choice of finish may have to be influenced by your working environment. If you are using lacquer, you must have some means of air extraction – necessary if you are using a brush, but absolutely vital if you are spraying. When using oils, always unfold the cloths and preferably put them outside to dry. Oily cloths

Anatomy of a workshop
1 Finishing room; **2** compressor and spray gun; **3** exhaust fan; **4** main entrance; **5** saw horses; **6** manmade boards; **7** small fittings and consumables; **8** lumber storage; **9** bandsaw; **10** hand tool storage; **11** workbenches; **12** table saw; **13** thickness planer; **14** pillar drill; **15** power hand tools; **16** dust extractor.

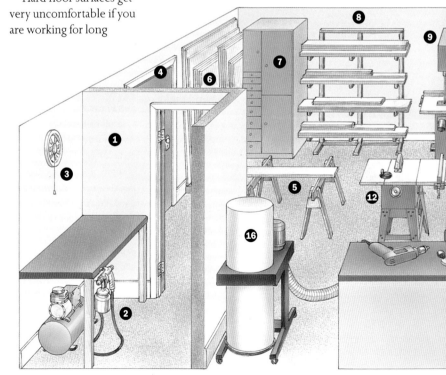

left in a bundle can self-ignite.

Dust extraction

When spraying, the air must be free of dust. Machining and sanding generate a great deal of dust. If possible, make sure that all machines are connected to a dust extractor. Wear a face mask when spraying or doing dusty jobs.

Light

One of the most important considerations is light. A good source of natural light is best, backed up with carefully placed sources of artificial light. Tungsten light is preferable to fluorescent, with individual spotlights over the workbench and over some of the machines.

Heat

Your workshop should be heated to just under the temperature of the place where the piece of furniture will finally be

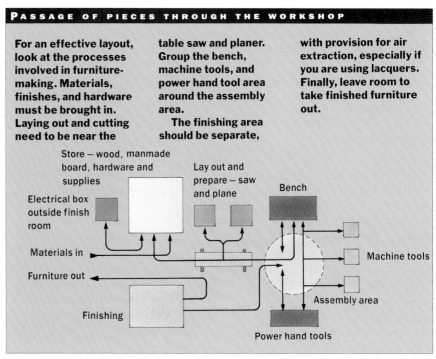

PASSAGE OF PIECES THROUGH THE WORKSHOP

For an effective layout, look at the processes involved in furniture-making. Materials, finishes, and hardware must be brought in. Laying out and cutting need to be near the table saw and planer. Group the bench, machine tools, and power hand tool area around the assembly area.

The finishing area should be separate, with provision for air extraction, especially if you are using lacquers. Finally, leave room to take finished furniture out.

Store – wood, manmade board, hardware and supplies

Electrical box outside finish room

Materials in

Furniture out

Finishing

Lay out and prepare – saw and plane

Bench

Machine tools

Assembly area

Power hand tools

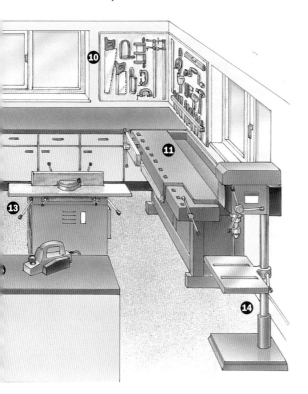

situated. Furnituremakers working in cold and damp workshops have had work ruined by wood movement when it has been taken into a centrally heated environment.

Scrap and waste

You will often have small pieces of wood and other materials that can come in handy for subsequent jobs. Anything of a respectable size is worth putting in a special place where you can reach it easily.

What is not usable scrap is waste – shavings, sawdust, etc. Sweep up daily, since waste on the floor is a potential hazard.

Safety

Keep the work space neat. Have a fire extinguisher and first-aid box attached to a wall where they are in plain view of anyone coming into the workshop. Install a smoke alarm.

Delivery

Make sure you can get finished furniture out of the workshop into the car, trailer or van, and into its final location. Large pieces may need making in sections for final construction or delivery.

FURTHER INFORMATION	
9	Safety first
16-19	Basic hand tools
50-53	Advanced hand tools
76-77	Power hand tools
92-93	Machine tools

Principles of Frame Construction

With cabinet and chair construction, the frame is the basis for many pieces of furniture. Some chairs are basic frames; most tables are either open or closed frames (a table with four legs and top rails only is an open frame). Frames are found in doors, and some cabinets can be based on frame construction. In fact, the idea of frame and panel construction gives a very economical way of making furniture, since thin panels will make light frames quite rigid.

In England during World War II, Utility furniture was developed to give quality products with very economical use of materials. Unfortunately, its potential was not fully exploited after the war.

FRAME DEVELOPMENT

Early furniture used logs, but as woodworking developed, wood was converted into boards and then into squares or rectangles. Some early furniture is obviously board-derived. However, it was found that strong constructions could be achieved by using wood as vertical and horizontal frame members. Furniture today still follows these basic principles. Some different frame applications are shown on this page.

Chairs
Some early chairs and some very simple modern chairs make use of the frame. The number and width of rails help improve the structure, and of course the insertion of a panel will further help, for example, in Jacobean panel chairs. ▲

Tables
The table is either a closed or open frame. A small coffee or display table is quite strong at this scale, and the top is a great help in keeping the frame square. With dining tables, however, there is always the problem of fitting knees under the top rail and the wish to maximize leg room. ▼

Doors
Doors are one of the most common ways where frames are reinforced by panels. ▲

Cabinets
A cabinet can be made using a light frame and thin panel construction. It is true this is a cheap method of manufacture and is often found in production furniture, but the principle is sound, and good furniture can arise from delicate use of this system. ▼

Built-in furniture
The front frame that holds the doors of large cabinets is a good example of frame construction. It is essential to make sure that when the frame is inserted, there is a means of checking and making it square so that the doors will work properly. ▼

PROBLEMS OF FRAME CONSTRUCTION

The development of the frame gave rise to the mortise and tenon joint, but the square or rectangle is not an integrally strong basic structure. In order to make the right angle strong, it needs triangulation, and it is this that most forms of construction try to accomplish.

Strengthening methods

One way of strengthening a square frame is to make one or two of the members as deep as possible so one thicker rail holds the whole structure. ▼

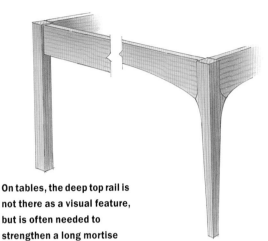

On tables, the deep top rail is not there as a visual feature, but is often needed to strengthen a long mortise and tenon. As an alternative to a deep rail, the rail may be thickened toward the joint, with a gunstock-shouldered mortise and tenon. ▲

Another, and simpler, way of adding maximum strength is by inserting a panel within the frame. This principle is used in many pieces to solve the problem of right-angled joints. ▶

Another method is a combination of deep rails and panel inserts. Braces or triangular pieces in the corner of quite a light frame will add enormous strength. In open shelving systems, diagonal bracing on the back is often used to serve the same function. ▶

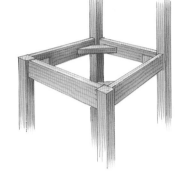

Strengthening right-angle joints

There are two specific solutions to the problem of strengthening a right angle. Traditionally made chairs have corner blocks in each of the four corners. These of course support a drop-in seat, but their job really is to keep the frame square. ▶

To achieve fine table legs without sacrificing leg room, one way is to reinforce the legs, triangulating them back up to a member across the top. ▼

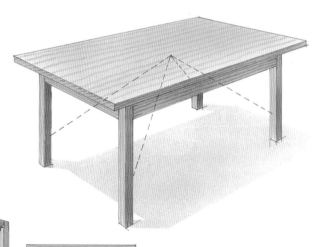

The Principles of Cabinet Construction

Cabinets were traditionally made from solid wood. The wood could be left natural, veneered, polished, stained, or lacquered.

During this century, advances in manmade board have produced plywood, particle board, chipboard and MDF. Construction techniques for manmade materials call for a different approach.

CABINETS IN SOLID WOOD

The main fact to bear in mind is that wood moves. There is hardly any movement along the grain, but a surprising amount of movement across it, and all cabinetmaking techniques using solid wood seek to allow for this.

Cross-grain movement varies with the wood, its moisture content, and conditions in which it is used. Controlled heat and humidity tend to stabilize the wood at a particular stage, but changes in moisture and humidity mean the wood will move markedly. It can vary between $1/50$ to $1/100$ of the width, i.e. ⅛ and ¼ inches in a 12 inch width.

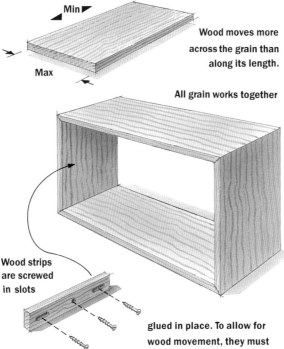

Wood moves more across the grain than along its length.

All grain works together

Wood strips are screwed in slots

Carcass construction

By constructing a cabinet with the grain direction running around it, the whole cabinet works together, any movement being from back to front. Strips of wood running across the cabinet, from front to back, cannot simply be glued in place. To allow for wood movement, they must be screwed to the sides. Insert one screw in a hole; the other screws in slots. Make sure that the length of this cross strip is reduced so that it will not contact backs or doors. ▲

Panel construction

When inserting solid wood into a frame, the panel must be allowed to move within the groove. Either leave the panel free and do not glue, or put a spot of glue in the center of the panel so that the sides can move. ▶

Allow frame to move in the groove

Back construction

The same procedure is necessary for backs of cabinets, which can be solid wood or plywood. ▼

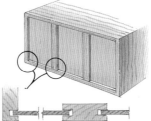

Cabinet back inserted into grooved frame

Table tops

The same principle is found in solid table tops where strips of wood are screwed to the underside to keep the top flat. Designer/craftsman Alan Peters cuts this strip in the form of a dovetail, which gives a beautiful visual detail in his table. ▼

Slot-screwed wood strips keep table tops flat

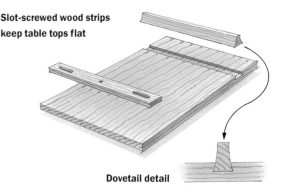

Dovetail detail

Muntin for wide boards

Grain direction in drawers

Drawers

Drawers must also follow this principle on grain direction. Plywood drawer bottoms present no problem, but with solid wood, the grain direction should run side to side, with the screws holding the bottom to the back in slots to allow for the movement. ▲

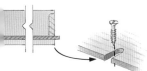

Slot- screw the bottom

MANMADE BOARD

Manmade board is inert, and any movement will be in all directions; therefore, jointing systems can be much simpler.

Mitered box with splines or biscuits

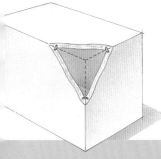

KEEPING CABINETS SQUARE

Cabinets must be kept square. Distortion can lead to joints failing and doors and drawers jamming. Corner joints alone are rarely enough to hold a cabinet rigid.

Box base

Strengthening the base

A five-sided box at the base of the cabinet acts in a similar way to the principle of a wide rail in frame construction. If the box is strong and rigid and the sides firmly secured, this will give the whole cabinet rigidity. ▲

Plywood or frame and panel back

Strengthening the back

Many cabinet designs rely on the back for rigidity. This can be a sheet of plywood sliding into grooves or rabbets or a frame and panel. ▲

Strengthening the interior

A cabinet with shelves and drawer runners. Grain direction of all pieces must allow for movement of the wood. Runners are slot-screwed in place. ▼

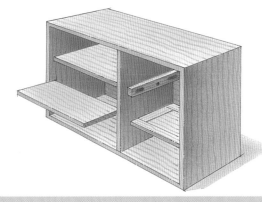

A variety of joints can be used. In solid wood, decide whether you want the joint to be decorative and to show. Corner joints can be through dovetails; shelf joints can be through multiple mortise and tenons.

If you do not want the joints to show, but want to practice cabinetmaking, use single half-blind, blind, or secret miter dovetails for corner joints. Use tapered dovetail dadoes for shelves. However, as long as you remember to allow for grain movement, the cabinet can be joined with splines or biscuits.

Manmade boards will be covered with a veneer or paint finish, so all joints can be hidden in the miter: dowels, splines or biscuits. Simple butt joints will be glued and nailed or screwed if you wish to finish with filler and paint. Screws or nails must be recessed and covered with filler.

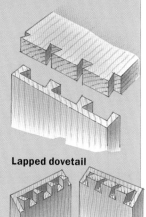

Lapped dovetail

Secret or miter dovetail

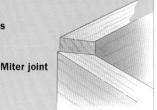

Miter joint

Finishes

A finish is applied to wood to improve its decorative qualities and to protect it from the elements and from general use. The choice of finish will depend on the nature of the piece you have made, the characteristics of the wood, and the situation in which the piece will be used.

There is a wide choice, and the decision as to what to use will be made on practical considerations of protection or on how to enhance the appearance of particular wood. With some woods it is quite suitable to leave the wood without a finish, especially where it is used indoors; however, a finish does enhance most woods.

TYPES OF FINISH

A finish has either a low or high build, or thickness. It is unusual to leave wood completely natural. However, you may wish to use a very low build finish, such as oil or wax. These enhance the nature of the wood, give some protection, and allow the natural character of the wood to predominate. However, dirt will easily get into the grain, and the pores and the finish will have to be regularly attended to, added to, or sometimes stripped and re-applied from scratch.

You can apply a higher build finish which seals the wood grain but does not completely encapsulate the wood. You can see and feel grain through finish. There are times when you wish to fill the grain completely and apply a high build finish so that you can see the wood color and pattern, but not feel the texture.

A finish can either be flat, satin, or high gloss. The higher the gloss required, the more build of finish has to be applied; therefore, you have to use fillers and several coats of lacquer, sanded between each coat.

Wood can be left without finish. Simply rub very fine steel wool over the wood for a flat surface. For a satin finish, use steel wool with wax polish. For a very high build finish, use lacquer and rub it so that it gives a high gloss encapsulation of the wood.

1 Linseed oil
Linseed oil takes several weeks to dry between coats, but the finish is very durable.

2 Tung and Danish oils
Tung and Danish oils have added chemicals to hasten drying.

3 Beeswax
Beeswax is natural wax which needs regular attention if used alone.

4 Paste wax polish
Paste wax polish is generally best applied over a finish and not used alone.

5 Clear lacquer
Clear lacquer can be sprayed or, if thinned, brushed on. May be a one or two-part type.

6 Polyurethane varnish
Polyurethane varnish is a synthetic resin that is easy to apply and hard-wearing.

7 Wood stains
Wood stains are useful if you want to enrich a wood that has

an undistinguished color (for example, some of the mahoganies) or to use a positive non-wood color (for example, primary colors).

8 Shellac
Shellac is a constituent of French polish. It gives a beautiful finish, but is damaged by heat and moisture.

9 Brushes
Brushes to apply finishes range from cheap to expensive. All need care in cleaning and storage.

10 Aerosol cans
Aerosol cans are useful for small jobs. They may be cellulose or acrylic, but are expensive for large jobs.

11 Cloth and cheese cloth
Cloth and cheese cloth are used to make a pad to apply French polish and oils.

WOOD TYPES/APPROPRIATE FINISH

You can use any finish on any wood, but some lend themselves better to particular finishes.

Fumed oak: Ammonia fumes color wood containing tannic acid. Oak turns golden to dark brown. Add a clear lacquer finish to protect the color.

Mahogany – high gloss: Mahogany traditionally has a high build and high gloss finish. It often needs staining to enrich the color since few mahoganies available today have the depth of color of Cuban mahogany used in the 18th and 19th centuries.

Oiled teak: Teak's natural properties make it resistant to rot and insect attack and is ideal for an oil finish.

Ash-matt lacquer: Ash has an interesting grain and it is preferable not to add a high build finish. A matt finish is more appropriate.

Waxed walnut: Walnut is a lovely timber which looks good when waxed. With dark woods white waxes are not always appropriate so buy a wax of a darker color.

Waxed walnut

FURTHER INFORMATION	
9	Safety first
19	Basic hand tools: sandpaper
71	Finishing
89	Using a spray gun

Wall-Hung Cabinet

The finished appearance of this small wall-hung cabinet is deceptively simple. The cabinet sides are joined to the top and bottom with secret miter dovetails. The dovetail joint is completely hidden by the mitered shoulders and its construction is a real test of accurate laying out and cutting. The back consists of a panel fitted into a grooved mortise and tenon frame.

A rabbet cut around its outside edge allows the back frame to slot neatly into a matching groove in the cabinet.

The shelf is tongued into blind dadoes cut in the sides. Finally, the completed cabinet is cleverly and neatly suspended from the top rail which is beveled to rest on a wall-mounted board.

AIMS OF THE PROJECT
Introducing secret miter dovetail joints.
Making a frame and panel construction.
Making blind dado joints.

TOOLS YOU WILL NEED
Chalk
Pencil
Ruler
Panel saw
Marking gauge
Craft knife
Jack plane
Dovetail saw
Range of chisels
Mortise gauge
Try square
Power router or plow plane and a hand router
Bar clamps
Cabinet scraper
Sanding block

TIME TO ALLOW
Allow plenty of time for this project if you are new to woodworking. You will need at least three or four weekends.

REMEMBER
When cultivating new skills such as cutting dovetails, or any joint encountered for the first time, make one or more samples first, before working on the main wood.

HEALTH AND SAFETY
Follow the safe working procedures outlined on page 9.

CHOOSING WOOD
It is possible to use almost any of the quality furniture hardwoods for this project. Choose a wood that is neither too hard nor too soft. Maple, ash, or beech would be appropriate from among the light-colored wood; mahogany would be a suitable red wood, and walnut a darker choice.

Softwood is not recommended because precise, clean cuts are essential for well-fitting joints.

No	Sawn	Planed
	CUTTING LIST	
2	SIDES 2ft x 11in x 1in	1ft 10in x 10in x ¾in
1	TOP 1ft 5in x 11in x 1in	1ft 3in x 10in x ¾in
1	BOTTOM 1ft 5in x 10in x 1in	1ft 3in x 9¼in x ¾in
1	SHELF 1ft 3in x 10in x ¾in	1ft 2in x 9in x ½in
2	FOR FRAMED BACK STILES (UPRIGHTS) 2ft x 1¾in x 1in	1ft 10¼in x 1½in x ¾in
2	RAILS 1ft 4in x 2½in x 1in	1ft 2in x 2in x ⅞in
1	WALL BATTEN 12in x 1¾in x ½in	11in x 1⅜in x ⅜in
1	BACK PANEL manmade board approx. 1ft 7in x 12in x ¼in	

+ masking tape, finishing, adhesive, 2 screws for cabinet back, wall fixings for batten

PLANS

The drawings on this page and overleaf show the elevations and sections, together with an exploded perspective view of the finished piece.

Scale 1:9

Back slides up from bottom in grooves on sides and top

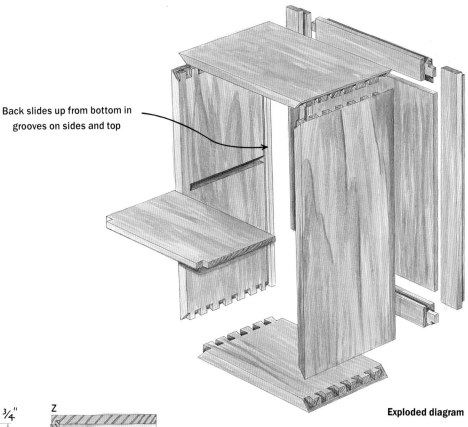

Exploded diagram

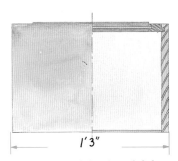

1' 3"

Sectional half plan through A-A

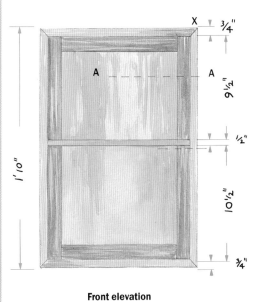

1' 10"

X   3/4"

A ———— A   9 1/2"

1/2"

10 1/2"

3/4"

Front elevation

Z

10"

Sectional side elevation through center line

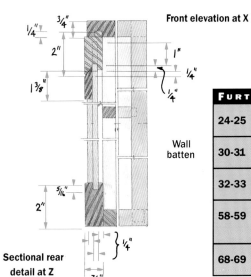

3/4"

1/4"   2"

1 3/8"

1"

1/4"

1/4"

5/16"

2"

1/4"

7/8"

Wall batten

Sectional rear detail at Z

Front elevation at X

FURTHER INFORMATION	
24-25	Planing
30-31	Reading drawings
32-33	Basic joining
58-59	Principles of cabinet construction
68-69	Making dovetail joints

BUYING WOOD

1 Most of the wood for this job could be prepared from 1 inch thick rough sawn boards.

2 Lay out all the components on the board in chalk and carefully saw them.

PLANING ALL COMPONENTS

3 Plane the face sides and face edges. Apply face and edge markings. Gauge and plane the width, then gauge and plane the thickness.

LAY OUT THE CABINET

4 Lay out the main cabinet parts, the two sides, the top, and the bottom. You will see from the drawing that the bottom is slightly narrower than the other three components, since the back will slide up in a groove from the bottom of the cabinet.

5 Mark overall and shoulder lengths in pencil. Mark the shelf position. Check all marking before you begin any cutting.

6 Cut the grooves in the sides and top to accommodate the back panel. This will be an easy job if you have a router, or use a plow plane. ▲

CORNER JOINTS

7 The joints on this cabinet could be either miters using dowels, splines or biscuits, or dovetails using through dovetails, half-blind, full-blind or secret miter. For this project, "bite the bullet" and make a secret miter dovetail. It is important that you practice this joint on scrap wood before doing it on the main carcass.

8 Pay particular attention when laying out to the junction between the two sides and the bottom at the back, because instead of a miter in this position, the sides must be kept square.

9 Mark the shoulders on the inside faces. Mark the miter on the edges. You must remove wood from both parts of the joint in the form of a rabbet across the end. The wood that is left represents the dovetail pins and tails. As is normal practice, the dovetails will be on the sides and the pins on the top and bottom.

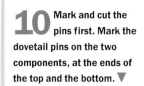

10 Mark and cut the pins first. Mark the dovetail pins on the two components, at the ends of the top and the bottom. ▼

11 Cut the pins and remove the waste by a series of saw cuts and by paring with a chisel. ▼

12 Mark the tails onto the sides, but before doing so, letter or number each joint clearly. Working on one joint at a time, mark the precise position of the tails from the pins. Be sure to pencil in the waste that you wish to remove. ▼

13 Remove the waste from between the tails, using a dovetail saw and chisel.

14 The dovetails on the bottom corners can now be tapped together, the dovetails on the secret miter will only fit partially together, but you can check and adjust at this stage. ▼

15 The secret miter joints will not come tightly together until you have cut the miter on the front faces, on the rear faces and across the corner. When this miter is cut you should be able to tap the dovetail together. ▶

16 Assemble the cabinet dry at this stage and check that the joints fit. ▲

SHELF

17 The total length of the shelf includes the dado depth. Mark in pencil a ¼ inch shoulder all around both ends of the shelf. Check that the shoulder lines are precisely the width of the shoulders on top and bottom. ▼

18 Now saw the shoulders and finish with the shoulder plane. ▼

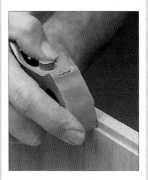

19 Disassemble the cabinet and mark the dadoes, first in pencil, then with scribe lines. In this first job, it is advisable to have a shoulder all around, even though dadoes can be made bare-faced or with a dovetail on one edge.

FURTHER INFORMATION	
70	Holding and clamping
86-87	Using a router

20 Cut the dadoes in the sides. Check the shoulder length, and mark and cut the tongues to fit the dadoes. ▼

21 Again, reassemble the whole carcass dry and check it for squareness at the corners and diagonally. ▼

22 Apply bar clamps to determine the best sequence for assembly. Generally with this type of cabinet joint, you should only need to clamp the tails into the pins from side to side.

23 Disassemble, clean up the insides of the cabinet and all around the shelf, mask the joint surfaces where they will be glued, and apply a finish to the inside.

24 Remove the masking tape from the joints, apply the glue and clamp the carcass, remembering to check again for squareness.

25 When the glue has cured, sand the outside of the carcass and apply the required finish. ▼

BACK FRAME

26 Lay out the back components. This is a simple frame with mortise and tenon joints at the four corners. Since the frame is grooved to hold the plywood panel, the haunches on the tenons are square, rather than sloping as on the Small Table, so that they fill the groove. ▼

27 Cut the groove for the plywood panel on the inside of the frame components using a router. Notice that the top rail is thicker than the two stiles. This is so that the cabinet carcass will be held away from the wall when the top rail is positioned on the wall-mounted board. ▶

28 Mark and plane the bevel on the top rail where the support board will fit. When marking, remember that the extra thickness is on the outside of the back frame, refer to the full-size detail drawing for clarity, and double-check all laying out before cutting.

29 Cut the mortises and haunched tenons, having first checked your marking yet again.

30 Mark the back panel out on the plywood. Check your marking, cut and fit the panel into the back frame. Assemble the frame and panel dry, clamp and check for squareness.

31 The back frame has a rabbet cut around the outer edge which allows it to slide into the back of the cabinet. Cut this rabbet now. ▼

32 If all is well, glue the back, checking it for squareness and twisting. Remove the clamps when the glue has cured. Check that the back slides into the cabinet. ▲

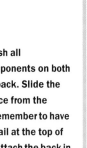

33 Finish all components on both cabinet and back. Slide the back into place from the bottom up. Remember to have the beveled rail at the top of the cabinet. Attach the back in the cabinet with two screws at the bottom. ▼

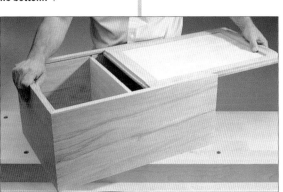

34 Make the wall boards, and plane the bevel to fit the top rail.

Attach the board to the wall ▼

35 The finished cabinet brings together a number of classic cabinet-making techniques. ▶

Making Dovetail Joints

For many furniture makers, the dovetail is a pleasurable joint to make since it is both decorative and a display of skill. It holds two pieces of wood together, normally at a cabinet or drawer corner. One part of a dovetail joint consists of the tails and the other part the pins. There are other ways of making corner joints as described below, but the through dovetail joint is a real demonstration of a woodworker's skill, and this is the joint shown in this technique.

Dovetail proportions are generally judged by eye to give a balanced and attractive result. Note the arrangement of pins and tails on narrow rails or wide boards. Draw the proportions of the dovetails on a piece of paper, then decide which to make first: the pins or the tails. For through dovetails, either way is acceptable, but when you begin making half-blind, full-blind and secret miters it is much easier to make the pins first and mark the tails from them, so this system is used here.

Preparation

There are two methods of working: either make the dovetails exactly to the correct length or make them so that the pins and tails project past the face of the wood, which is then planed down. The best method is to make the joint to the correct length from the start, as this is necessary in several applications shown later. Prepare the two pieces of wood, exactly planing the face side, face edge, marking them and then planing width and thickness and carefully squaring both ends.

The wood

The through dovetail is generally used for the corners of cabinets, boxes, or drawers, so any convenient size softwood will do. Two pieces of wood 8 inches long by 4 inches wide by ¾ inch thick will be suitable.

Proportions

Different ways of arranging dovetail proportions are shown below. Generally, the pins are finer than the tails. Angles must not be too great, leaving short grain on tails, nor too shallow to be effective.

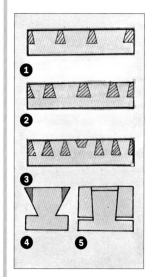

Types of dovetail
1 Even spacing.
2 Tails grouped at the sides.
3 Decorative and functional.
4 Too much slope.
5 Too little slope.

MARKING THE PINS

1 Set the cutting gauge to the thickness of the wood and then gauge around one end of each piece from the end to mark the shoulder line. ▶

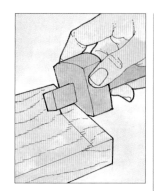

2 Put one piece in the vice, gauged end uppermost. Using a sliding bevel, mark the pins in pencil, and shade in the waste to be removed. When you are sure you have it right in pencil, mark cut lines on the end surface with a knife. Later, if you make many dovetail joints, you may make or buy a dovetail template. ▶

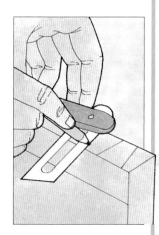

3 Using a square and a craft knife, mark down from the end of the dovetail lines. ▶

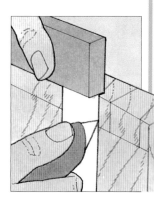

CUTTING THE PINS

1 With a dovetail saw, carefully saw to the waste side of the line down to the shoulder line. ▶

2 Saw out the waste with a coping saw, making sure the saw cut is about 1/16 inch from the shoulder line. ▼

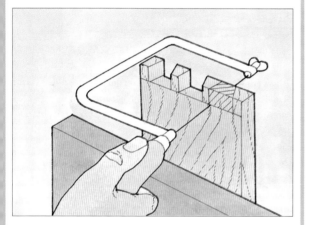

3 Pare down to the shoulder at the gauge line, working from each side so as not to split the surface of the wood. There should now be a series of nice crisp "holes" for which you have to make some tails. ▶

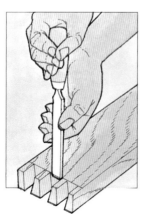

MARKING TAILS FROM THE PINS

1 Lay the piece of wood which is to have the tails on the bench face side up, and place the piece already cut in the position in which it is to fit. Put the craft knife against the side of the pin, and make a cut line. ▼

2 Shade the waste areas. Check here that you have marked this correctly and then, using a square and a knife, cut the lines across the end of the wood. ▼

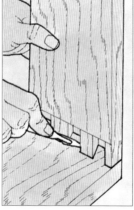

CUTTING THE TAILS

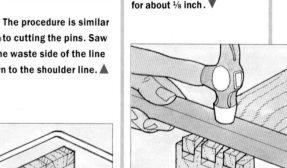

1 The procedure is similar to cutting the pins. Saw to the waste side of the line down to the shoulder line. ▲

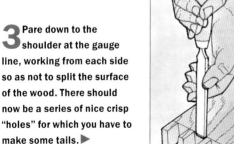

2 Now saw out the waste with a coping saw and, as previously, chisel to the shoulder line. ▲

FITTING THE TWO PARTS

1 The joint should fit the first time. However, as this is a first attempt, put the piece with the pins in the vice, pins uppermost, and place the piece with the tails in position. Protecting the outside of the wood with a piece of scrap wood, tap the joint together for about 1/8 inch. ▼

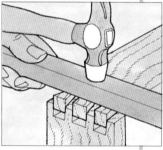

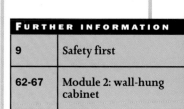

2 See how the joint is fitting and decide if any chiseling is necessary to make the joint fit. The interference between any two parts will show when the joint is taken apart. Pare carefully, making sure you do not take off too much, and fit the joint which should now be able to be tapped home.

FURTHER INFORMATION	
9	Safety first
62-67	Module 2: wall-hung cabinet

Holding and Clamping

When you use any clamps, always make sure the face of the work is protected by using a small pad of scrap wood under the clamp faces. It is often convenient to attach these protective blocks in place on the clamp heads with masking or double-sided tape first.

To make a wide board from narrower widths, use bar clamps to exert pressure on the joint, positioning them on both sides of the board.

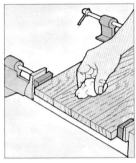

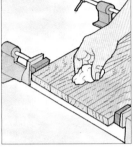

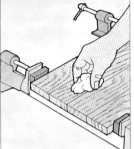

1 Lay the bottom clamps on the bench, glue and gently squeeze the joints together. Wipe away any excess glue squeezed out of the joints. ▲

2 Locate the upper clamps and tighten all clamps. This will ensure that the boards do not spring, but stay flat. Such surfaces can be glued only, or you can use dowels, tongue and groove, or biscuit joints. ▲

CLAMPING A FRAME

1 Bar clamps ensure joints are tight when clamping a frame. Check the frame is not twisted by sighting from rail to rail, from stile to stile or leg to leg. ▼

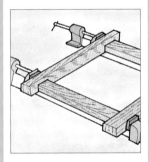

2 Check the frame is square by using a try square and by checking the diagonals. If the frame is out of square, move the clamps as shown to correct it. ▼

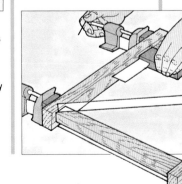

CLAMPING A MITER

There are two methods. Use four bar clamps and tighten very carefully to make sure the miter closes. This method is fine when the miter is doweled since the joint cannot slip.

However, if tongues or biscuits are used, slipping can cause problems, and the alternative method is better. Glue softwood triangular cheeks to the outside of the frame corners (shown above). This enables the clamps to apply pressure all along the joint.

When the glue is cured, saw off the cheeks and plane the edges. ▲

CLAMPING A CABINET

The principles of clamping and checking are similar to those applied when clamping a frame. The operation can be very complex, however, requiring many clamps.

It is essential that cabinet assembly is carefully planned and that you have a dry run without glue first, before the final assembly with glue.

USING A BAR CLAMP IN A VICE

Grip the bar clamp in the vice, using scrap wood on each side of the clamp. Use this technique to hold long work, or for example, when planing square boards to a cylinder or making faceted (hexagonal or octagonal) components. ▼

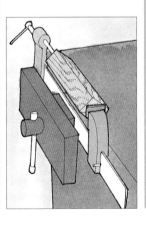

Finishing

The finishes available are summarized earlier in this book. You must first decide which finish is appropriate to the completed work. This decision depends upon the nature of the piece and how and where it is to be used. For table surfaces, a hard lacquer may be best, but on certain chairs oil is preferable. Before applying any of the finishes discussed below, the wood surfaces must be well prepared by planing, scraping, and sanding.

APPLYING OIL WITH A CLOTH

Using a clean, soft cloth folded into a pad, wipe the oil on the wood. Do not over-apply. The surface should not be swimming in oil; any oil that has not been absorbed into the pores should be wiped off after a few minutes.

Apply a series of light coats rather than heavy ones. Oil is a finish that needs time to build up. There is a saying: "Apply once a day for a week, once a week for a month, and once a month for a year." ▶

APPLYING ONE-PART LACQUER WITH A BRUSH

Do not attempt to apply thick coats, but brush the lacquer on thinly and allow it to soak into the grain (shown above). When the lacquer has hardened, cut it back with fine silicon carbide paper. Work through the grits of sandpaper to the very finest available. Make sure the surface is dust-free before continuing with applications of lacquer. Finally apply a coat of paste wax and buff to a sheen. ▲

APPLYING TWO-PART LACQUER WITH A BRUSH

1 Mix the hardener (catalyst) with the lacquer to the proportions recommended by the manufacturer, usually one part of catalyst to nine parts lacquer. ▶

2 Mix only enough for the work at hand, since any left over becomes like jelly and then hard and cannot be used. Apply thin coats of lacquer with a brush. Cut back between each coat as described above for one-part lacquers. Subsequent applications will build to a good hard-wearing finish. ▶

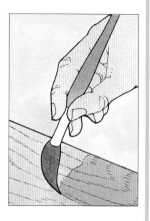

3 After the final application, for a "satin" finish, apply a wax coating (see "Applying wax", right) or, for a high gloss finish, the surface can be rubbed, either by mechanical buffing or by using automotive rubbing compounds. ▶

MAKING A HOLDER FOR A MOP OR ROUND BRUSH

A mop is an expensive and specialized tool, and many furnituremakers make a holder specially for it from a glass jar with a metal screw top filled with lacquer thinner or cleaner. Cut a hole in the metal top and push the handle through so the bristles are suspended in the thinner. This keeps the mop in good condition and always ready for use. ▼

APPLYING WAX

Wax is best as a final finish for oils or lacquers. Apply the wax with a cloth, or with the finest grade of steel wool in a very thin film. Leave for a while, then buff with a soft dry cloth.

FURTHER INFORMATION	
9	Safety first
60-61	Finishes

Cabinet

The basic cabinet consisting of four sides and a back can be varied in many ways. Solid wood sides joined with dovetails is the classic traditional method shown in Module 2.

Joints can be hidden, or they can be visible, contributing to the appeal of the finished piece. The carcass can be of solid wood, or a frame and panel construction as used for the desk in Module 6. Manmade board can be used and combined with modern machine joining methods.

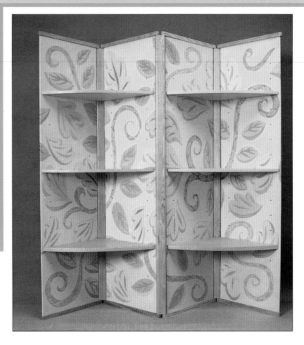

SHAPE AND SIZE

Cabinets can be made in a variety of different shapes and sizes, depending on what they will hold and the space available. Large cabinets stand on the floor to become bookcases or cupboards.

A cabinet can also be combined with other furniture – standing on a table, for example. Cabinets of different proportions can also be combined to make more elaborate pieces of furniture such as dressers or hutches.

A wall-hung cabinet, if it is to carry heavy loads, must be securely installed. You can give extra support by screwing a batten to the wall for the cabinet to rest on, as well as hanging the cabinet from the top.

Floor-standing cabinet

Wall-hung cabinet

LEE SINCLAIR • *Shelving screen*
Made in painted MDF and ash, this clever combination of a screen and shelves gives an added dimension to a room divider. The panels were decorated by Cynthia Harrison using acrylic paint then sealed with clear lacquer. ▲

Proportion

Make a scale drawing of the front elevation to consider variations in the proportion of your cabinet designs. The shape should look right in terms of proportion and balance, and you can also use the drawing to check that the cabinet will hold all the objects you want to store.

A long design may need extra support in the middle.

A tall design may not be stable and may need attaching to the wall, even if it is floor-standing. ▶

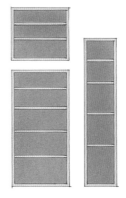

Inside the cabinet

A cabinet interior can be arranged in many different ways, too. Shelves can be varied in number and proportion, or they can be combined with drawers. ▼

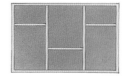

Shelves can be fixed or adjustable. Adjustable shelves increase the versatility of the cabinet. It will improve the rigidity of the cabinet if at least one central shelf is fixed. ▼

A display cabinet, where the pattern of the shelves forms an important part of the design calls for careful planning. The shelves could be made from a contrasting wood to the outer carcass. ▼

DOORS

A door or doors can be added to the cabinet, or you could choose to include some areas of open shelving. Doors can be made using a frame and panel to allow for movement in the wood. With manmade boards, doors can be made as a single sheet.

A single door opening on a simple hinge is the most basic form. ▼

Double-hinged doors are hinged in the same way, but the central break down the front of the cabinet creates a very different look. ▼

Sliding doors must run in grooves inside the cabinet. These can either be routed out, or you can buy pre-formed plastic tracks to screw into the cabinet. For large or heavy doors, buy a specially-made roller mechanism combined with track and glide mechanism for the bottom of the door. Sliding doors are useful in a restricted space, but only half the cabinet is accessible at any one time. ▼

Folding and sliding doors allow access to the whole of the cabinet interior. The doors must be mounted on a readymade roller-guide system. ▼

Fold-away doors need compartments at the side with enough room to take each door. ▼

Vertical folding doors, including rise and fold and fall flap doors, require specialized hardware. Before you consider a design using these features, check that you can buy the required hinges. ▼

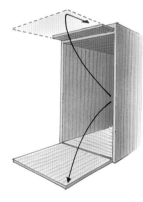

Instead of doors, for an entirely different design approach use a paper screen, shades or blinds to cover the front of a cabinet. ▼

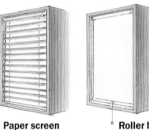
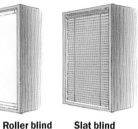

Paper screen   **Roller blind**   **Slat blind**

NIC PRYKE ● *Display case*
This elegant piece for displaying objects was specially commissioned by a museum. The delicately tapering oak legs are bleached and sandblasted. The patinated copper shelves have been subjected to heat and a chemical process which causes the coloration. ◄

These projects take you further into furnituremaking. Module Three, nursery furniture, introduces the techniques used in working with manmade board. It is easier to use than solid lumber, but the basic skills covered earlier are essential: planning and marking accurately. You will easily be able to adapt the use of this material to your own designs. Module Four, the small chest, introduces drawer making and includes a variation on cabinet construction, using machine joints. Drawer making is a very good combination of skills, and you will use it again in other jobs. This section also introduces chair making with a simple but original design using shaped solid wood to give interest on the seat and back. The chair has joints that show and add to the effect of the entire piece. On completion of these modules, your skills will have developed well, giving you a springboard to more complex projects.

Power Hand Tools

Even though it is important to develop a feel for wood by using hand tools, their machine equivalents are immensely valuable.

Power hand tools are not only useful for removing the drudgery of routine tasks, but results can often be achieved much more quickly and easily than by hand. The router and biscuit jointer particularly are the power tools that really give the ability to carry out work that would otherwise require a lot of skill and specialized hand tools. You must always follow all the safety rules when using these tools.

the router to perform as a dovetail machine. Once you have become familiar with the machine, you will find its only limitation is your imagination.

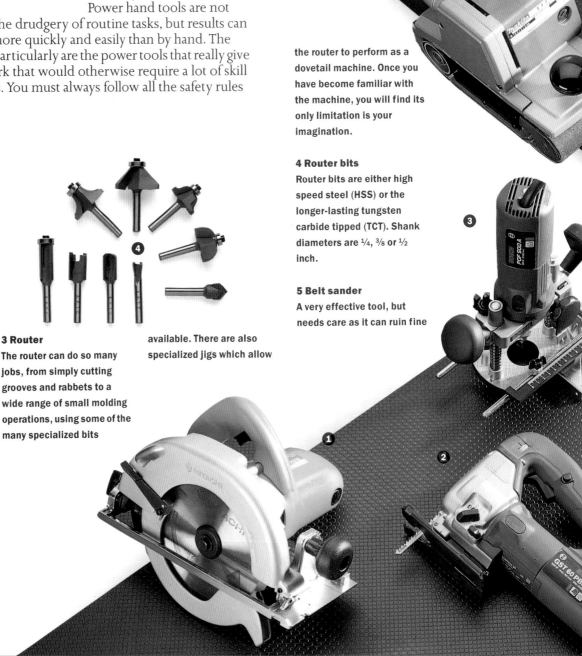

1 Circular saw
The circular saw can cut either along or across the grain and can be used as a machine held in the hand or inverted on a specially designed frame to make a miniature table saw. Always take great care to make sure that it is fully guarded at all times and that you are very methodical in its operation.

2 Jigsaw
One of the first power tools to buy, since it is so versatile. It can make straight cuts with or across the grain as well as free-shaped cuts. It is good for jobs ranging from cutting out to quite substantial shaping work. Initially, it is a good substitute for a bandsaw and a fretsaw. With care it can cut wood up to 2 inches thick. It can accept a variety of blades, and can even cut thin sheet metal and plastic laminate.

3 Router
The router can do so many jobs, from simply cutting grooves and rabbets to a wide range of small molding operations, using some of the many specialized bits

available. There are also specialized jigs which allow

4 Router bits
Router bits are either high speed steel (HSS) or the longer-lasting tungsten carbide tipped (TCT). Shank diameters are $\frac{1}{4}$, $\frac{3}{8}$ or $\frac{1}{2}$ inch.

5 Belt sander
A very effective tool, but needs care as it can ruin fine

work by taking off too much wood. It is preferable to use the plane, the scraper, and sandpaper. The belt sander,

however, is useful inverted in a stand where it can be used for sanding and shaping small items.

6 Drill

Probably the oldest of the electric tools, long used by hobbyists. It is preferable to have at least a couple in different sizes, one small battery-powered machine for fine work and a larger electric-powered one. Very good jigs are available to convert the tool into a drill press.

7 Orbital sander

A good aid to final finishing, but do not start with too coarse a grit – as the plate moves in an orbit rather than in a straight back and forth motion, this machine can put marks into the wood. Use hand methods first and only use this machine with approximately 120 grit or finer. When you have a lot of sanding to do, however, it does relieve a lot of very hard work, and the better models can produce very acceptable results.

8 Planer

The planer can remove a lot of the hard work from wood

preparation, when it is best used held in the hands. It can also be inverted and installed in a stand to act as a small jointer. You can achieve a large measure of accuracy this way, but you must remember to follow the safety instructions very carefully.

9 Biscuit jointer

A fairly recent development which is largely used to substitute for dowels and splines. It is a very effective machine for cutting the precise hole needed to accept the specially prepared biscuit inserts, and it makes cabinet jointing very easy. It has the advantage that it can be used both on solid wood and on manmade board.

10 Battery pack and charger

More and more tools are battery – rather than electric – powered. Recent advances in technology have seen the rates at which battery chargers operate fall from 16 hours to 5 minutes.

FURTHER INFORMATION	
9	Safety first
32-33	Basic joining
86-87	Using a router
88-89	Biscuit joining
130-131	Power planing

Spraying

Finishing can be completely carried out by hand methods, but there may be occasions when you wish to apply paint, stain, varnish, or lacquer with a spray gun. Once you have mastered the technique, spraying gives a perfectly even finish. There are two main spraying methods: air spraying, where the finishing liquid is atomized with compressed air; and airless spraying, where the finish is compressed to atomize it and no compressed air is needed.

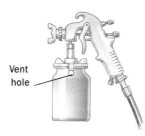

Vent hole

ENVIRONMENT
You need an area which can be separated from the working space, to prevent the mist that forms during spraying (overspray) from contaminating equipment and work in progress. An exhaust fan is necessary to remove fumes and overspray, as is some form of noninflammable curtaining or partition to separate the space. If much has to be done, you will probably need to invest in a specialized spray booth.

You will need to make some form of rotating platform upon which the work will stand and some form of racking or shelving so that finished work can dry or cure.

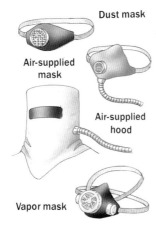

Dust mask

Air-supplied mask

Air-supplied hood

Vapor mask

you will need some form of mask. The simplest is a dust mask, but for some finishes, a vapor mask may be necessary. With a lot of spraying, you may need an air-supplied mask, or an air-supplied helmet or hood, both of which provide an independent air supply. ▲

Compressed air-assisted spraying
An electrically powered compressor delivers filtered air to a spray gun. The compressor consists of a pump or motor, a tank into which the air is delivered and stored (with a relief valve and a means of draining off surplus water), a condenser to clean and dry the air, and a regulator to provide constant airflow at a preset pressure. Several different types of spray gun may be used with compressed air. ▼

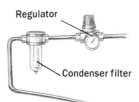

Regulator

Condenser filter

Siphon or suction spray gun
This finish reservoir is attached underneath the gun's grip. As the compressed air passes through the gun, suction pulls liquid up and delivers it to the spray head. ▲

Gravity-fed spray gun
The finish is held in a small cup on top of the gun, and enters the gun by gravity. A useful gun for a home workshop. ▲

Airbrush
This can be used for very small jobs. It provides precise control and is only worth considering if you have a small, precise job to do and can borrow or rent one. ▼

Pressure-fed spray gun
The paint or lacquer is held in a pressurized container so the finish is delivered to the gun under pressure. It is convenient to use since there is little weight in the handset, but it is limited to large-scale spraying operations rather than the home workshop. ▼

Safety
Most finishing materials are flammable and potentially explosive when sprayed as a fine mist in air. There must be no naked flames or lights. Do not smoke!

The fumes given off by spraying can be harmful, and

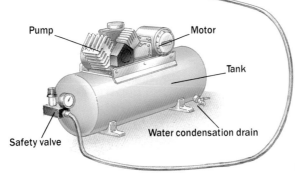

Pump

Motor

Tank

Water condensation drain

Safety valve

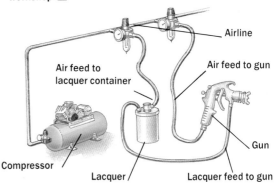

Airline

Air feed to lacquer container

Air feed to gun

Gun

Compressor

Lacquer

Lacquer feed to gun

Atomizing the finish

However the finish is delivered to the gun, it is at the nozzle that the material is changed from a fluid to a spray, and there are two types of mixing cap to do this job.

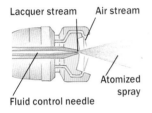

Lacquer stream   Air stream

Fluid control needle   Atomized spray

External mixing cap

The liquid stream is ejected from the gun nozzle, and the compressed air atomizes the liquid into a spray outside the nozzle. It gives accurate control of the spray pattern, since airflow can be adjusted, and is good for fast-drying lacquers. ▲

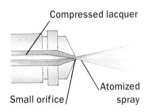

Compressed lacquer

Small orifice   Atomized spray

Internal mixing cap

Generally used with airless equipment, the liquid is pressurized inside the cap, the spray shape and pattern being determined by the shape of the nozzle orifice. ▲

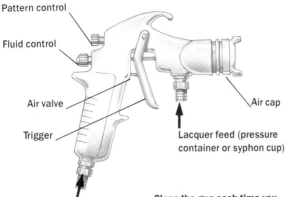

Pattern control

Fluid control

Air valve

Trigger

Air cap

Lacquer feed (pressure container or syphon cup)

Air feed from compressor

Adjustment and cleaning

Controls on the gun adjust delivery rates of air and finish. The air flow adjuster controls the rate of air flow: high flow for thicker material, lower for thinner ones. This can sometimes be controlled at the compressor rather than at the gun. The pattern control regulates the quantity of air flowing to the mixing cap, and this changes the spray pattern. The flow of material is controlled by adjusting the fluid control and amount of trigger movement. The procedure is – fill the lacquer container, spray and set the air flow adjuster, adjust the fluid control to obtain an even coat of finish, adjust the pattern control to give the required spread and shape and, finally, the pattern direction. ▲

Clean the gun each time you use it by spraying lacquer thinners through the system. Occasionally take the gun apart and thoroughly clean and reassemble. ▲

Airless spraying

The principle of airless spraying is that the finish is pressurized and forced out of the spray orifice in an atomized form. This system is limited to large equipment for bulk or industrial use, but there are a few adaptations for smaller users. ▼

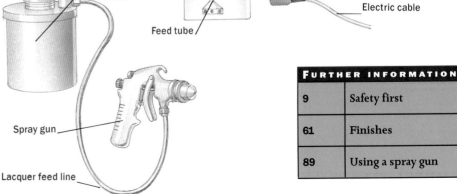

Pressurized container

Spray gun

Lacquer feed line

Electric spray gun

A small gun is available which follows the system described above, but on a scale suitable for home use. The results can be quite fair, but the disadvantage is that the finish has to be at a specific viscosity for it to be sprayed well. It must be thinned to a specific consistency using a viscosity cup. This is a measured container with a hole in the bottom, the contents of which must empty in a specific time. It is more useful for finishes that are near the correct viscosity, since over-thinning can affect some finishes. ▼

Internal mix cap

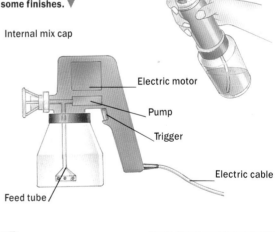

Electric motor

Pump

Trigger

Electric cable

Feed tube

Aerosol spray

Commonly available for automotive finishes, this can give good results but is an expensive way to buy paint. It may be difficult to find clear lacquer suitable for woodwork.

Glass jar aerosol

A glass jar, with aerosol top allows you to spray whatever finish you wish. It is necessary to use the fluid at the correct viscosity. ▼

Nursery Furniture

This nursery furniture is an ideal opportunity to explore the possibilities of working with manmade board using hand power tools. The construction is straightforward, the joints can be splined and grooved using a router or a biscuit jointer. The decorative possibilities are limited only by your imagination.

AIMS OF THE PROJECT
To give experience in cutting, shaping and joining manmade board.

TOOLS YOU WILL NEED
Coping saw, power jigsaw, or bandsaw
Power router or biscuit jointer
Pencil
Ruler
Marking gauge
Craft knife
Jack plane
Try square
Bar clamps
C-clamps
Sanding block

TIME TO ALLOW
Time lies in assembly since components are assembled in stages, and the glue must cure before moving on to the next stage.
It could take a couple of weekends to do the machining and joining, and a couple of weeks of work in the evenings joining components.

REMEMBER
Any manmade board needs one or more coats of sealer before applying the finishing color coat. Use sanding sealer or a primer/filler. Sealing and finishing coats can be brushed on, but if you wish, use this project to learn how to use a spraygun.

HEALTH AND SAFETY
Follow the safe working procedures outlined on page 9.

CHOOSING MATERIAL
MDF has been used here because it is so simple to finish; plywood or chipboard would do equally well.

With this project, the "cutting list" is in the form of a drawn layout, rather than a set of components so that you can reduce waste (see overleaf).

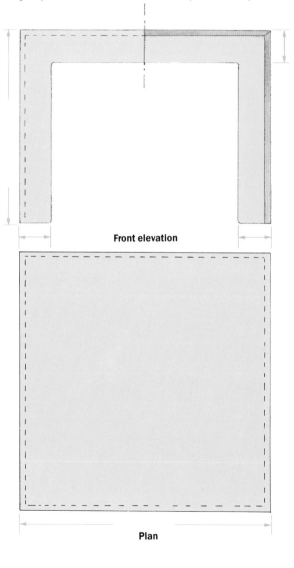

Front elevation

Plan

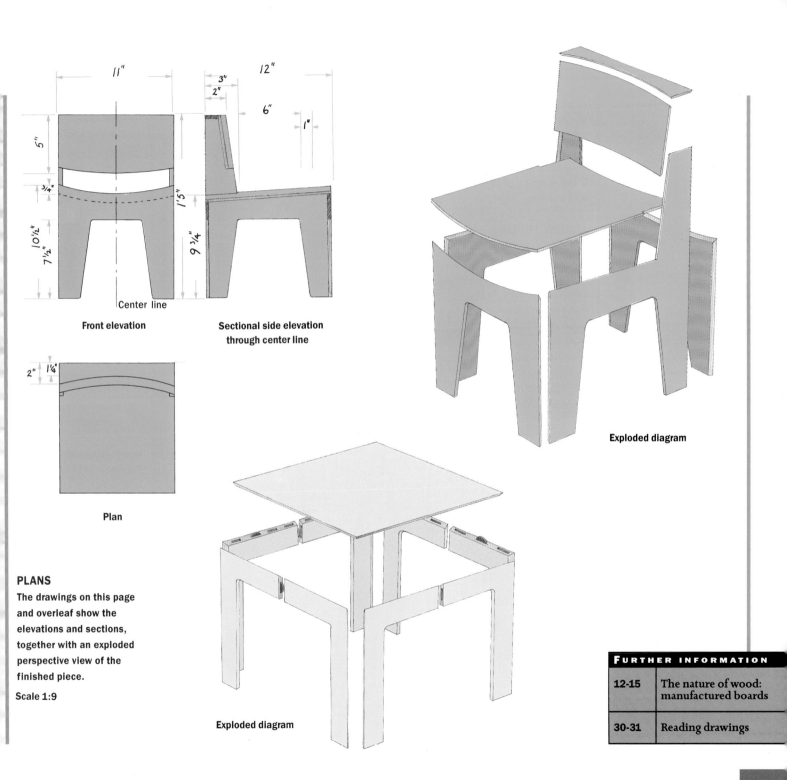

11"

5"

3/4"

10 1/2"

7 1/2"

Center line

Front elevation

12"

3"

2"

6"

1"

1' 5"

9 3/4"

**Sectional side elevation
through center line**

2" 1 1/4"

Plan

PLANS

The drawings on this page
and overleaf show the
elevations and sections,
together with an exploded
perspective view of the
finished piece.

Scale 1:9

Exploded diagram

Exploded diagram

FURTHER INFORMATION	
12-15	The nature of wood: manufactured boards
30-31	Reading drawings

MAKING THE TABLE

1 Follow the diagram to lay out components on the board. The board is cut in order to utilize the material as economically as possible. ▼

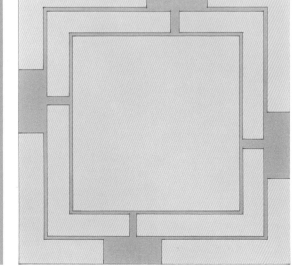

2 The legs are grouped around the table top. You will need either a coping saw or a power jigsaw to cut the L-shaped pieces for the legs. Clean up any rough edges with a sanding block.

JOINTING THE LEGS

3 The 8 L-shaped pieces are mitered together in pairs to form four leg-and-rail corner components. To fit these to the top, you can either miter the top and the tops of the corner components, or set the legs directly under the top. The project is described using miters all around.

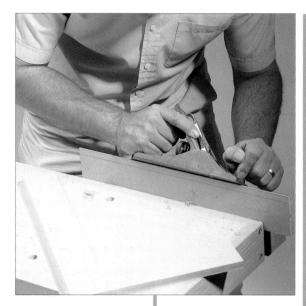

CUTTING MITERS

4 Plane a 45-degree miter all around the table top, and also around the outer edges of the eight L-shaped leg components. Alternatively, cut the miters using a router. ▲

MAKING THE JOINTS

5 Set the router with a small cutter ($3/16$ inch) and cut grooves for the splines along the mitered surfaces. You will need to cut splines from a piece of plywood of the same thickness as the grooves. ▼

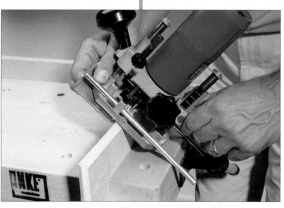

6 Alternatively, use a biscuit jointer to make short grooves for biscuits.

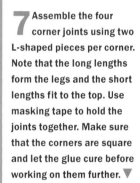

7 Assemble the four corner joints using two L-shaped pieces per corner. Note that the long lengths form the legs and the short lengths fit to the top. Use masking tape to hold the joints together. Make sure that the corners are square and let the glue cure before working on them further. ▼

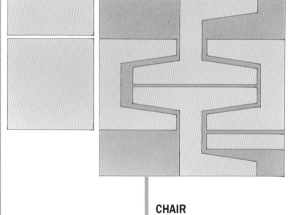

8 Take two leg assemblies and glue them to the top on opposite corners. The geometry of the joint should mean that everything will be square when these joints are glued and clamped together. Again, let the glue cure before going on to the next stage. ▲

9 With the first legs in position, fit the final pair. Not only will you be jointing legs to the top, but you will be jointing the rail between each leg section. Glue these last two leg components in position, and when the glue has cured, your table structure should be finished and very strong.

10 The corners of the table are very sharp, however, and you will need to plane the outside edges. For small children, a larger rounded edge may be preferable, and this is a chance to use the router with a round-over or other specially-shaped bits.

11 Now sand the table all over in preparation for the sealing coat. MDF needs slightly less sealing than either chipboard or plywood, but any manmade board needs one or more sealing coats before applying the finished color coat. Sand lightly between each coat. ▼

12 Apply the finishing coat or coats in the color you have chosen. Next apply any decorative effects you have. This project used "falling letters," but you will no doubt think of a variety of ways of adding interest.

CHAIR

13 Lay out components on the board as shown in the diagram. Two thicknesses of board are specified: $3/8$ inch for the main chair frame and $1/8$ inch or $3/16$ inch for the seat and back. If you are making more than one chair, you will probably be able to use the material more economically. ▲

14 Cut the components from the board, using a jigsaw.

FURTHER INFORMATION	
47	Preparing the surface
76-77	Power hand tools
86-87	Using a router

19 Assemble the frame dry, adjust, and check. If all is well, glue the frame, the two sides, the back and front, and the top rail, and let the glue cure. ▶

15 Plane all components to the required shape. It is easiest to make all the edges square at this stage. Pay attention to the sloping angle on the inside edges of the legs. ▲

16 Cut the miters on the four corners of the main sections. Stop the miter on the back leg above the seat at the position shown and also at the top corner where the top rail fits.

17 Cut rabbets for the seat and the back rest. ▲

18 Make splines and grooves or biscuit joints.

20 If you have used thin material for the seat and back, it will bend to the curve easily. MDF (¼ inch) was used for making the prototype and the seat and back shapes had to be pre-curved before fitting. If you need to do this, clamp the pieces in a rough jig, having cut the seat and back very slightly over-size. ▼

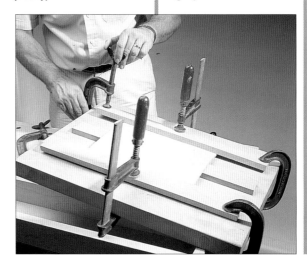

21 You will then need to fit the seat in position, and it is a tricky piece of measuring to get it to fit precisely. The seat fits in the rabbets on all four sides, except at the rear where it is cut away to fit inside the side frames. ▼

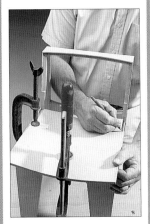

22 When the seat fits, dry, glue, and clamp in position. ▼

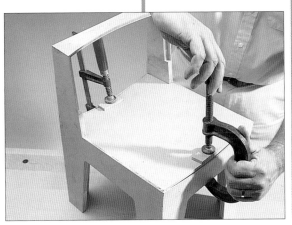

23 The same, but slightly easier procedure, applies for the back rest. Fit and glue in position. ▲

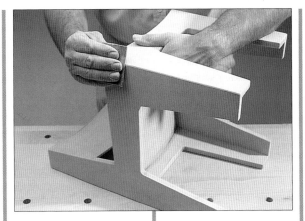

24 Now, as with the table, sand off sharp edges or use a router with a round-over bit. ▲

25 Finish the chair using the same procedures that were used for the table. Use filler if necessary, sand all over, apply sealing coats and the finishing coat. ▲

26 The finished table and chair decorated with "falling letters." ▼

FURTHER INFORMATION	
60-61	Finishes
70	Holding and clamping
78-79	Spraying

Using a Router

The router is a useful tool and has become popular with woodworkers because it can do so many jobs that were once the province of specialized tools such as rabbet planes, plow planes and molding planes.

INSERTING ROUTER BITS

1 Use a wrench to tighten the collet so that it grips the router bit firmly. Some machines have a spindle lock, others need a pin through the spindle to immobilize it while you tighten the collet nut. ▼

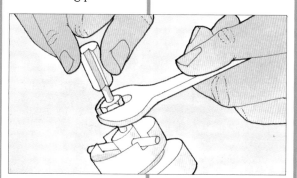

2 If your router does not have a collet nut, use two wrenches, one to grip the spindle and one to tighten the collet nut. Arrange the wrenches in a V-formation so that you can squeeze them in one hand. ▼

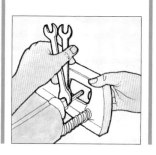

USING A ROUTER

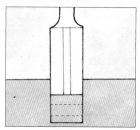

1 To prevent the wood from burning and to lengthen the life of your bits, make a series of shallow cuts, rather than attempting to make one deep cut. As a general rule, only cut to a depth equal to half the bit diameter with any one cut. ▲

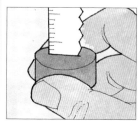

2 Most routers are of the plunge type, and you can set the depth of cut in advance, using the depth stop. Some routers have rotating multi-depth stops so that you can set the range of cuts for the job. The router illustrated has three threaded stops in a revolving holder to give a sequence of cutting depths. ▲

3 Router bits rotate in a clockwise direction, so as the machine is pushed forward, it has a tendency to pull to the left. In cutting a groove with the fence on the right-hand side, the router's leftward pull holds the fence firmly against the work. ▼

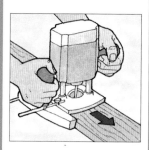

4 To operate the plunging router, make sure that the bit is locked in a raised position above the work. Position the router where you want to begin the cut. Switch on the router. ▼

3 Router bits rotate in a clockwise direction, so as the machine is pushed forward, it has a tendency to pull to the left. In cutting a groove with the fence on the right-hand side, the router's leftward pull holds the fence firmly against the work. ▼

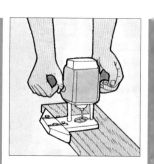

5 Loosen the plunge handle to plunge the bit into the wood as far as the depth stop. Move the router forward to make the cut. Keep the router moving steadily. Moving too fast may overload the motor, too slow may burn the work and damage the bit. With experience, the sound of the motor is your best guide. ▲

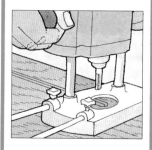

6 At the end of the cut, loosen the plunge handle and let the bit retract from the work. Then switch off. This is the basic freehand process. ▲

ROUTING GROOVES

1 To cut a groove parallel to the edge of the wood, use the straight fence supplied with the router. Mark the position of the groove on the wood and adjust the fence so that the bit runs parallel to the edge. For a deeper cut, make a series of passes. ▶

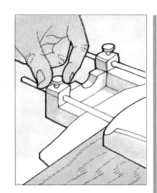

2 Use a batten as a guide to cut a groove on a wide board, or a groove that is not parallel to an edge. Mark the groove position, measure from the bit to the edge of the router base, and clamp the batten this distance from the groove. Run the router against the batten. ▶

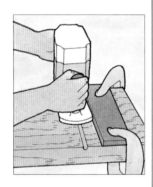

3 To cut a wide groove in the middle of a board, use two battens. Position each one so it allows the router to cut the sides of the groove, then rout out the center. ▶

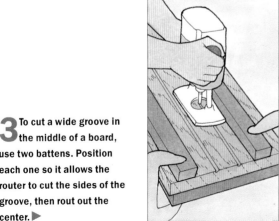

ROUTING RABBETS, CHAMFERS, AND PROFILES ON EDGES

1 Molding and edging bits have a guide pin or a ballbearing guide which runs along the edge of the wood below the rotating bit so that the bit can be used without a guide fence. ▼

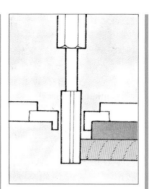

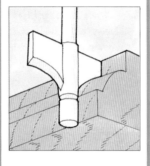

2 If the work is straight and not too wide, shape the edge by running the guide fence along the opposite side. ▼

3 To cut shapes and edges, use a template and a guide bushing. The guide bushing is screwed into the router base. It allows the router to follow the edge of a template. The size of the guide bushing relates to the bit diameter. There should be an ⅛ inch gap between the bit and the guide. ▲

4 Make the template from MDF or plywood. Roughly cut the workpiece oversize and secure the template to it with double-sided tape. Run the guide bushing along the edge of the template, taking a series of cuts, if necessary, to shape the edge of the work. ▼

Biscuit Joining

The biscuit jointer is a power tool that has been developed to make an alternative to traditional edge and butt joints such as tongue and groove or dowel joints. The closest traditional equivalent is the loose tongue joint.

The biscuit jointer offers a simple, quick, and accurate way of making such joints in either wood or man-made boards. It is widely used in small-scale industrial workshops.

A biscuit joint is not as strong as mortise and tenon or dovetail joints and should not be used on the corners of frames.

The biscuit jointer itself is a small-diameter circular saw held safely in the body of the machine. The blade is plunged into the wood to make a groove for the biscuit in one cut.

The baseplate and guide fence mean the machine can be positioned accurately for the cut. There is also a bevel fence for cutting biscuit grooves in miter joints.

An insert made of compressed beech, shaped like a lozenge, a leaf, or a biscuit is inserted into the groove.

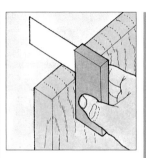

USING A BISCUIT JOINTER

1 First cut precise butt joints, either by saw or plane. Check both faces with a square to ensure they are at 90 degrees along their whole length. ▲

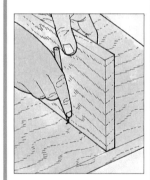

2 Mark the centers of the biscuits on both boards. Biscuits can be spaced with 2 to 3 inches left between each one. ▲

3 Set the jointer to make its cut in the center of the board's thickness. Holding the machine in position, switch it on and carefully make a plunge cut. Withdraw the blade without disturbing the position of the machine. ▶

"L" Joints

4 For "L" joints, leave the fence in position, and align the machine at the end of the second board. Make the cut. ▶

"T" Joints

5 For "T" joints, cut grooves in the board end as described in step 3 above. To cut the grooves in the second board, remove the guide fence, clamp a board or batten on the work, and align the machine against this to make the cut. ▶

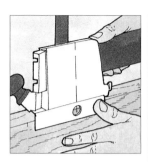

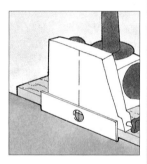

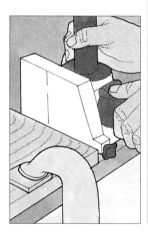

Using a Spray Gun

Joining miters

6 To join miters set the jointer to make its cut near the inside corner of the miter for greater strength. ▼

7 One method is to set the guide fence against the edge of the board to make the cut. ▼

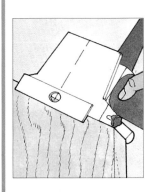

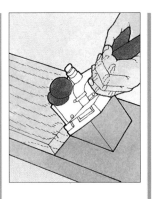

8 Alternatively, clamp the mitered board securely onto another board and rest the machine's bevel against the second board to make the cut. ▲

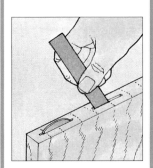

Assembly

9 To assemble the joint, use a thin wooden spatula to make sure glue goes right into the grooves. Glue the boards first, then fit the biscuits dry, and assemble. The biscuits swell when wet and grip in the grooves to add strength. Clamp the joint. ▲

Spraying should be done in a large, dust-free, well-ventilated room and in a good light. If you are spraying outdoors, choose a still, dry day.

Cover everything else in the vicinity with newspaper or a plastic sheet. For your own safety, wear a mask covering your nose and mouth.

SPRAYING PRACTICE

1 Before spraying, stir thoroughly with a stick, remove the stick, and hold it at a 45° angle. The liquid is the correct viscosity when it runs off in a steady stream. ▲

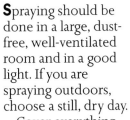

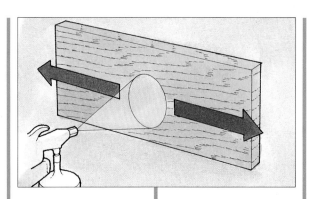

2 Practice first on scrap wood, experimenting with spray adjustment and distance from the work. Spray in smooth, steady strokes, keeping the spray at right angles to the work ▲

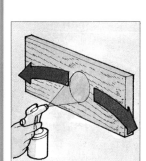

3 Do not spray in an arc, which results in uneven coating, and do not jerk the gun. Move the gun at a consistent speed so the thickness of the finish remains constant. ▲

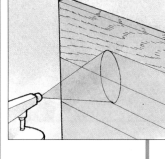

4 Overlap the strokes by about 50 percent, and spray past the ends of the work. Start moving the gun before you pull the trigger and release the trigger before stopping the gun at the end of a stroke. ▲

FURTHER INFORMATION	
9	Safety first
60-61	Finishes
76-77	Power hand tools
78-79	Spraying

MDF and Color

Manmade boards are immensely versatile to use to create simple furniture. With power and machine tools, they can be quickly cut to shape and joined to make furniture for children from babies to teenagers.

The basic techniques of working MDF and other manmade board can be applied to making a whole range of nursery furniture, including cupboards and desks as well as table and chairs.

Manmade boards also take paint and other decorative finishes so well that a wide variety of decorative ideas can be applied, from variations in color and texture, to complete fairytale scenes.

The whole approach to working with manmade board is different from solid wood, since the problem of wood movement does not exist. This gives the opportunity to design and construct forms that can only be successfully made in these materials. To investigate possible structures in manmade board, make scale models from cardboard as well as sketches.

GETTING STARTED

Once you have mastered the basic joining and finishing techniques, the only limit is your imagination. Children's furniture provides the ideal opportunity to exploit the versatility of manmade board.

ROBERT VENTURI ●
Colored chair
Manufactured boards can be shaped and joined successfully in ways that just would not work with solid wood. The asymmetrical back and fresh coloring give this chair a lively look, while its splayed legs make it sturdy and stable. ▲

ROBERT VENTURI ● *Table*
Each of the legs faces in a different direction, giving the table the same lively feel as the chair. Spattered and sponged paint needs little artistic ability, but is a very effective way of working with colors. ◄

JOHN ANDERSON • *Sea chest*
An opportunity to use laminating techniques to make the waves. The full sails and waving flags are detailed touches that add to the jaunty appearance. The paint effects, though simple, are also applied with attention to detail. ▶

ROBERT VENTURI • *Chair*
Seat and front legs are cut from one piece and bent at right angles, making a smooth curve. The glossy black finish enhances the bright paint. ◀

JAKKI DEHN • *Child's bed*
The chest of drawers base is practical and gives stability; large industrial castors are added for mobility. The paint effect – a simple pattern on alternate stripes – can be adapted to any color scheme. Note "tail" for suspending a mobile. ▲

FURTHER INFORMATION	
80-85	Module 3: nursery furniture

Machine Tools

Powerful modern machinery allows you to do precise work at a speed and on a scale that few home woodworkers would have attempted when only hand tools were available. Always treat machines with a great deal of respect and never use a machine when you are tired or affected by drugs or alcohol. Also never be tempted to do a job on your own when you really need someone else to support the work, for safety. If you do not take risks, these tools will save you much time and be a pleasure to use.

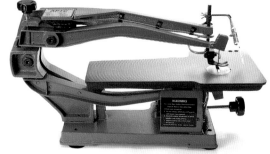

Scroll saw

The scroll saw can make very fine internal cuts on a complex shape, making it a fairly specialized machine associated with model-making more often than furnituremaking. However, good-quality machines will cut quite thick wood, and there is a large range of blades to choose from. A very fine cut can be achieved needing little or no subsequent sanding. ▲

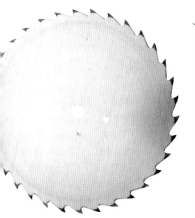

Saw blades

Saw blades are designed for a variety of jobs, from ripping to crosscutting; some also give a very smooth finish. It is always worth buying blades with tungsten carbide tips. They are more expensive and need to be professionally sharpened, but they stay sharp much longer. ▲

Radial arm saw

Not only sawing, but grooving, rabbeting, and shaping can be achieved with this saw. The blade can be rotated and angled in many directions to allow miters and bevels to be cut. Some woodworkers are devotees of this machine, others are not entirely convinced of the safety aspects of some operations, but used intelligently and sensitively, it achieves useful results. ▶

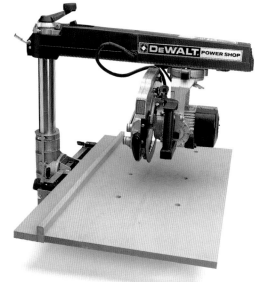

Table saw

The table saw is the first choice of machine tool for many woodworkers. It allows you to rip and crosscut with speed and accuracy. It will also cut grooves and rabbets.

However, it is essential for the blade to be properly guarded at all times. If you remove the top guard for any operations, make sure you take great care. ▼

Bandsaw

Both straight cuts, curves, and thick wood can be cut on this useful general-purpose machine. The blade is a fast-cutting continuous strip running over two or three wheels; its downward thrust means there is no danger of kickback. The bandsaw takes up little floor space, and the thin blade means little wood is wasted in the kerf. ▶

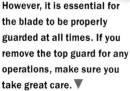

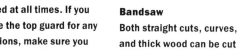

Jointer planer

This is the second machine to buy after the table saw. The saw cuts material. The jointer planer prepares it. For small workshops, the combination machine is excellent, and some good models are available. As with hand planes, the longer the table (or plane), the flatter and straighter the results. Most small machines have short tables and when using them check that you are achieving straight and flat work. After facing and edging wood with the jointer, the planer will size it to width and thickness. ▲

Drill press

This is the big brother of the power hand drill. Some woodworkers prefer a machine especially for mortises which can also drill, but a drill which can take a mortising attachment is preferable. The drill press generally has a wide range of speeds and is either floor- or bench-mounted with an adjustable table which can be raised or lowered. Floor-mounted machines allow you to drill long items. ▶

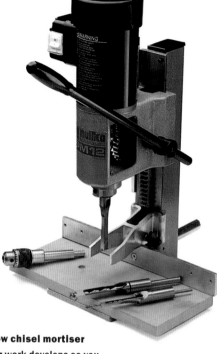

Hollow chisel mortiser

If your work develops so you have lots of mortises to make, this is a useful investment. The auger bit in the center cuts the hole, and the square sharp chisel is pressed into the wood to make a clean cut. Most home workshop models take square chisels $\frac{1}{4}$ to $\frac{3}{4}$ inch wide. ▲

Universal/combination machines

These machines generally include a table saw, spindle molder, jointer, mortiser planer, and sometimes a lathe.

At first sight, these seem an attractive proposition, however the universal machine is limited and you cannot upgrade freely.

Disk and belt sander

Generally, this machine is most useful for small-scale pieces, but be very careful since it can easily remove too much. You need a precise approach for good results. You can adjust the fence and the table on the disk sander for accurate smoothing of angles and end grain. ▶

FURTHER INFORMATION	
9	Safety first
54-55	Workshop planning
76-77	Power hand tools

Principles of Drawer Making

Drawers are boxes with an open top, designed to slide into a box with an open front, a cabinet. Drawers can be in a huge range of sizes and shapes, either to store and aid retrieval of specific objects, or to fit in with the proportions and details of a particular piece of furniture. Most drawers do both these tasks. These two pages look at how the drawer has traditionally been made and at alternative methods.

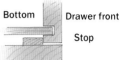

TRADITIONAL DRAWER CONSTRUCTION

The components of a drawer consist of the front, two sides, back, and bottom. The half-blind dovetails joining the sides and front tighten as the drawer is pulled out and so use the dovetails to contribute to the construction and strength of the drawer. The back is through dovetailed to the sides.

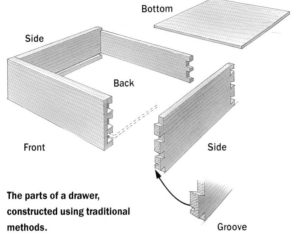

The parts of a drawer, constructed using traditional methods.

Wide drawers

Wide drawers often need the support of a central rail on the bottom, called a muntin. It is fitted with a tenon into the front and a notch at the back. The drawer bottom is made in two parts, each sliding into grooves in the side and the muntin. ▼

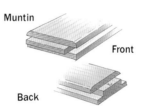

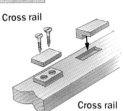

Cross rail

Drawer stops

A drawer should never be the full depth of a cabinet; if it fits flush between the sides and the cross rails, a drawer stop is needed. The easiest way is to screw or nail a block in place. The finer way is to inset an L-shaped block into a small mortise in the cross rail. ▲

Installing a drawer bottom

The bottom slides in grooves on the sides to a groove in the front. The back is cut high to allow the bottom panel to slide in underneath it. ▼

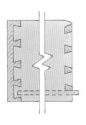

If a thicker drawer bottom, or one made of solid wood, is required, then it can be accommodated by chamfering the bottom around the edges. ▼

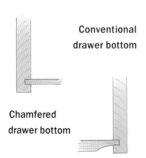

Conventional drawer bottom

Chamfered drawer bottom

Sometimes with fine, thin, drawer sides, there is not enough wood to cut a groove, so drawer slips are applied. These can be shaped, with a half round inside the drawer. ▼

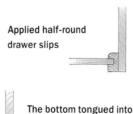

Applied half-round drawer slips

The bottom tongued into grooved slips

At the front, the slip has a tenon cut to fit into the front groove, and at the rear it is notched to fit under the back. ▼

Front

Back

The bottom is screwed at the back only, in a slot to allow for movement. ▼

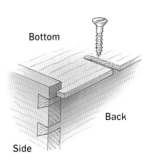

Fitting a drawer front

There are various ways in which a drawer front can be fitted into a cabinet. It can fit flush between the cross rails. An alternate flush-fitting method uses a small section of wood called a "cock bead" inset into the four front edges of the drawer front. This gives an interesting visual detail, but also makes the drawer slightly easier to fit than the previous method. Fronts can sit in front of cross rails, and this method has been used in the projects. Fronts can project above or below the cross rail. ▼

Short cuts in drawer making

A false front can be screwed onto a simple drawer. Use this method where the drawers cover the front of a cabinet, or to match the grain pattern in a series of fronts.

Other joints used to make drawers include the box or finger joint, which is quick to cut by machine and often used in commercial drawer making. A simple lap joint relies on the strength of the glue; avoid it unless the work is less than final. Miter joints strengthened with either splines or biscuits may also be used.

Sliding dovetails can join the sides to the front. Either a through or blind sliding dovetail will tighten up as the drawer is pulled out in the same way as through or half-blind dovetails.

A tray is a drawer with low sides. These can often be made with a simple frame, applying the bottom, flush or in a rabbet, with glue and nails or screws. It is possible to find commercially produced drawers, either in plastic, injection molded, or in the form of wire baskets. These items work well in kitchen. ▼

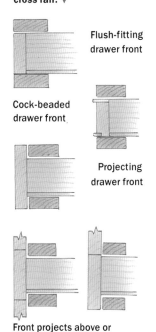

Flush-fitting
drawer front

Cock-beaded
drawer front

Projecting
drawer front

Front projects above or
below the cross rails

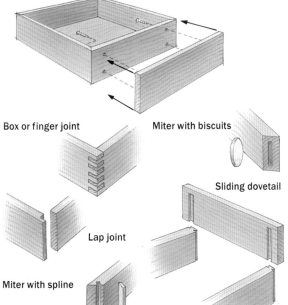

Box or finger joint

Lap joint

Miter with spline

Miter with biscuits

Sliding dovetail

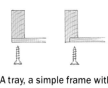

A tray, a simple frame with
bottom pinned or screwed
in place.

DRAWER RUNNERS

The traditional way is to insert drawer runners into blind dadoes in the cabinet sides. Runners are stub tenoned into the front cross rails, and no glue is used. Another common method is to make a blind groove on the drawer sides, cut a strip of wood to fit the groove, and then glue and screw the strip to the cabinet sides.

Runners glued and
screwed to the cabinet

To install a drawer under a surface or shelf, screw strips of wood to the drawer sides to run on strips screwed to the underside of the shelf.

A drawer suspended beneath a surface

Chest of Drawers

The next stage in cabinet construction after making the simple wall-hung cabinet is the making and fitting of drawers.

This cabinet contains four drawers, each of a different depth. The drawers are opened by finger grooves positioned so that they form a distinctive design feature across the cabinet front.

Classic fine furnituremaking techniques used in this chest of drawers include dovetail drawer joints, and dustboards between the drawers.

AIMS OF THE PROJECT
To give practice and build competence in making a set of drawers to fit into a cabinet.

TOOLS YOU WILL NEED
Chalk
Pencil
Ruler
Panel saw
Marking gauge
Craft knife
Dovetail saw
Range of chisels for dovetails
Mortise gauge
Mortise chisel
Try square
Power router
Biscuit jointer or drill depending on your choice of corner joints
Bar clamps
Cabinet scraper
Sanding block

TIME TO ALLOW
Depending upon the joints you use, the cabinet should only take two or three weekends' work. However, the new skill of making drawers will take more time to acquire.

REMEMBER
Treat this project in stages. First the carcass, second the interior parts and drawer runners and, third, the drawers. Precision is essential. The carcass must be square and the spaces for the drawers parallel.

HEALTH AND SAFETY
Follow the safe working procedures outlined on page 9.

CHOOSING WOOD

If you have made the other projects in order, you will now have experience in using both solid wood and manmade board.

The prototype was made from ash. For this first project making drawers, choose wood that is fairly easy to work. Beech is useful for the drawer sides and interior parts of the cabinet, while the drawer fronts and outside of the cabinet can be any wood of your choice.

CUTTING LIST: BODY		
No	**Sawn**	**Planed**
2	SIDES 2ft 3in x 1ft 1½in x 1¼in	2ft 2in x 1ft 1in x 1in
1	TOP 1ft 5in x 1ft 1½in x 1¼in	1ft 4in x 1ft 1in x 1in
1	BOTTOM RAIL 1ft 5in x 3in x 1in	1ft 4in x 2⅞in x ¾in
8	DRAWER CROSS RAILS 1ft 4in x 2¼in x ¾in	2in x ½in
8	DRAWER RUNNERS 8in x 1½in x ¾in	1¼in x ½in
1	CABINET BACK plywood 2ft 2in x 1ft 4in x ¼in	
4	DUST BOARDS plywood 1ft 1in x 8in x ¼in	
+ glue, finishing, screws		

CUTTING LIST: DRAWERS

DRAWER No 1 (TOP)

No	Sawn	Planed
1	FRONT 1ft 3in x 4¼in x 1in	1ft 2in x 4in x ¾in
2	SIDES 12in x 3¾in x ¾in	11in x 3½in x ½in
1	BACK 1ft 3in x 3in x ¾in	1ft 2in x 2⅞in x ⅜in
1	BOTTOM plywood 1ft 2in x 11in x ¼in	

The cutting list for the other 3 drawers is similar to drawer 1, but some parts change in width since the drawer depth increases. The widths are:

Sawn	Planed
2nd DRAWER Front 5½in Sides 4¾in Back 4in	5in 4½in 3⅞in
3rd DRAWER Front 6½in Sides 5¾in Back 5in	6in 5½in 4⅞in
4th DRAWER (BOTTOM) Front 7½in Sides 6¾in Back 6in	7in 6½in 5⅞in
+ glue, finishing, screws	

PLANS

The drawings on this page and overleaf show the elevations and sections, together with an exploded perspective view of the finished piece.

Scale 1:8

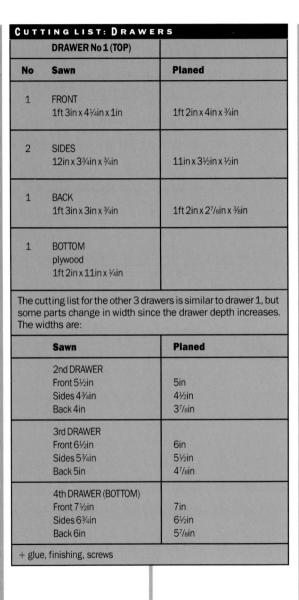

Center line

1'4"

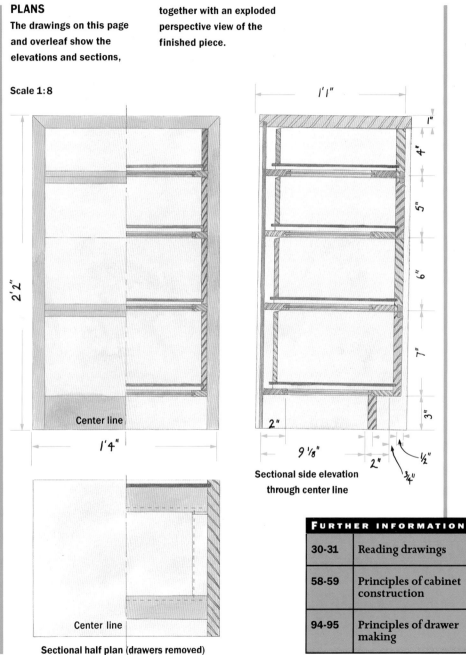

Sectional half plan (drawers removed)

Center line

2'2"

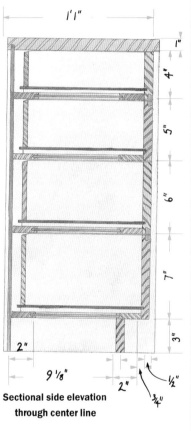

Sectional side elevation through center line

1'1"

1" 4" 5" 6" 7" 3"

9⅛" 2" ½" ¾"

2"

FURTHER INFORMATION

30-31	Reading drawings
58-59	Principles of cabinet construction
94-95	Principles of drawer making

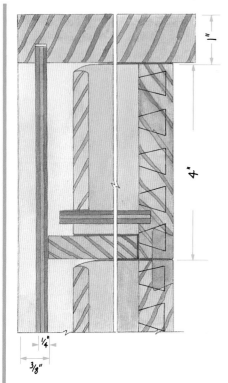

**Section showing detail of
cabinet and top drawers
Scale ½ size**

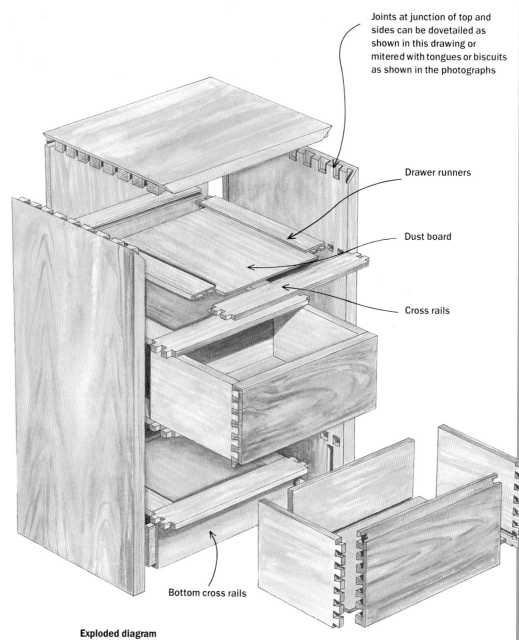

Joints at junction of top and
sides can be dovetailed as
shown in this drawing or
mitered with tongues or biscuits
as shown in the photographs

Drawer runners

Dust board

Cross rails

Bottom cross rails

Exploded diagram

BUYING WOOD

1 The top and sides are made from 1¼ inch wood, whereas most of the rest will come from 1 or ¾ inch wood. The back is made of plywood. Dustboards between the drawers are also made of plywood and the drawers have plywood bottoms.

2 Mark and cut out all components. Plane face side, face edge, width, and thickness, leaving slightly over length.

CARCASS CONSTRUCTION

3 Lay out the two sides and the top. The carcass consists of the sides and top, a bottom cross rail, and a back panel.

4 Make the corner joints. The wall-hung cabinet project used secret miter dovetail corner joints. Continue to practice by making dovetails on the top two corners or, miter these joints and use splines, biscuits, or dowels. This is an ideal project to use splines if you have a router.

5 It is essential to get a very good miter at these two corners. You will probably spend some time planing the miter and making sure that it is a good fit at 90°.

6 Rout the groove in the miter for the splines, or use a biscuit jointer. ▼

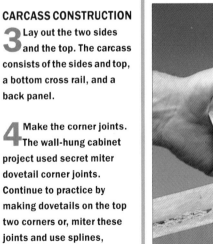

7 Place the tongue in the groove and fit the joint dry. ▶

8 Mark the bottom rail and make the joints that will hold it in place. The rail has a stub tenon fitted into mortises on the two sides. ▲

15 Lay out the components. ▼

9 Cut the groove for the back panel in the top and the sides. ▲

10 Cut and fit the plywood back. Its function is to hold the cabinet square and, as is normal practice, it slides into place from the bottom and will later be attached to one of the cross rails.

11 Sand the interior, then apply a finish if required (see 23).

DRAWER RUNNERS AND CROSS RAILS

12 Under each drawer is a frame consisting of a runner on each side and a front and back cross rail. A plywood dustboard is set within grooves cut on the inside edges of these pieces.

13 The front and back cross rails are glued in place. The runners and dust boards are slightly undersize from front to back. The runners are tenoned into the groove in the cross rails.

14 The design assumes that the sides are made from solid wood; therefore, there is likely to be wood movement. To allow for expansion and contraction, the tenon on the runners is fitted tight and glued at the front, while at the back the tenon and its shoulder are cut short about 1/8 inch to allow for any back to front movement in the cabinet.

16 Make stub tenons in the back and front cross rails and make corresponding mortises on the inside of the cabinet. Make sure that these shoulders are the same as those on the bottom cabinet rail. ▼

17 In order to fit the dustboard, cut the groove on the inside edges of the cross rails as shown in the drawing.

18 Fit the carcass together dry. Make any adjustments if necessary and take it apart again. ▶

19 Mark the positions of the front to back drawer runners on the inside of the sides. These are tenoned not into a mortise, but into the groove in the cross rails. ▶

20 Cut a groove for the dustboard in each runner.

21 Mark, cut, and fit four plywood dust boards.

22 Try assembling these components together. If all is well, check that all these internal components are sanded and that you can glue the carcass together. ▼

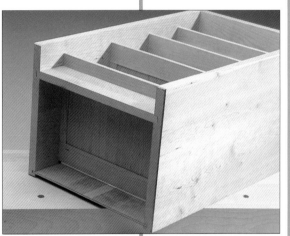

FURTHER INFORMATION	
70	Holding and clamping
86-87	Using a router

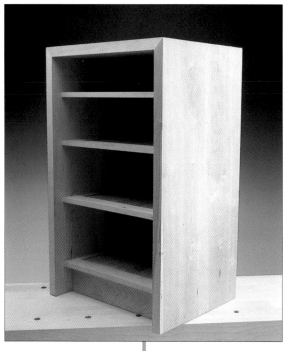

25 Each drawer back is not a tight fit vertically since it sits on the drawer bottom and does not extend the full depth of the drawer. It does, however, need to fit precisely across the carcass and you should be able to insert it from front to back. ▶

23 It is not usual to finish inside a cabinet with drawers, but you can apply a simple sealing coat of the chosen finish if you wish. Drawers should slide wood on to wood. You should now have a firm carcass structure in which to run the drawers. ▲

MAKING DRAWERS

24 Make and fit one drawer at a time, repeating the procedure for the other three. Plane the drawer sides so that they are an exact fit and slide in and out of the carcass. ▶

26 Take the drawer front and fit it into its opening. It should fit exactly on the inside face from end to end, but make a bevel so that it tapers toward the outside face, which is slightly longer. ▶

27 You will see from the drawing that the top drawer fits from the underside of the cabinet top to the lower face of the first drawer rail. ▶

28 Once sides, back, and front have been fitted, make the groove for the drawer bottom on the inside of the two sides and the front.

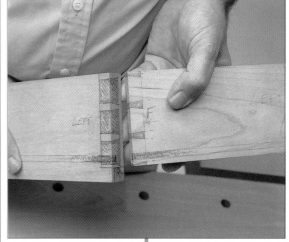

29 Mark the dovetail joints. Half-blind dovetails join the front to the sides. ▲

FURTHER INFORMATION	
68-69	Making dovetail joints
71	Finishing
94-95	Principles of drawer making

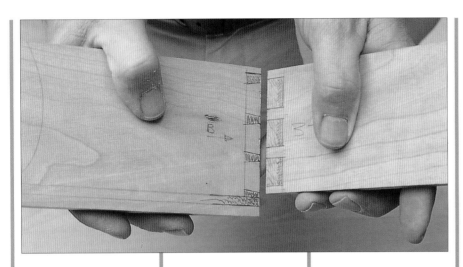

30 Through dovetails join the sides to the back. ▲

31 Remember to make allowances for the handle groove that is on the lower edge of the top drawer. The groove is on the upper edge of the second drawer, the lower edge of the third drawer, and the upper edge of the bottom drawer. When assembled, the grooves make a decorative feature running across the cabinet.

32 Cut the dovetails with care. Make sure that your gauge lines are precisely the thickness of the components. This technique does not allow for major planing of the drawer sides to ensure fit. The precise marking of the drawer back and front should mean that the drawer fits if the dovetails have been well made, with only a slight cleaning up necessary.

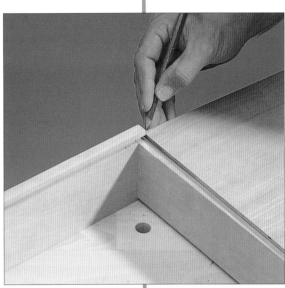

33 Mark the plywood bottom and cut to fit. ▲

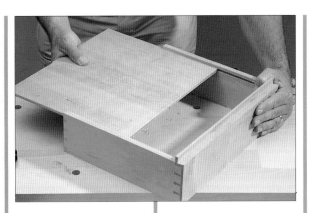

36 Now you have mastered drawer making on the first one, follow the same procedure for the other three.

34 Slide the bottom into place. The drawer bottom is not glued in the grooves; slot it in place and insert two screws at the back, through the drawer bottom up into the drawer back. Assemble the drawer dry and check that it is a tight fit. ▲

35 Add glue and assemble the drawer. When the glue has cured, it should only need a few touches of the plane to allow the drawer to run smoothly in its space. ▼

37 The cabinet back is attached with a couple of screws through the back into the bottom back drawer rail.

38 Sand the carcass and the drawer fronts, and apply the final finish.

39 The finished chest of drawers, waxed and polished — an asset to any room. ▲

FURTHER INFORMATION	
47	Preparing the surface
71	Finishing

Chest of Drawers

A cabinet to hold a set of drawers can be made almost any size or proportion, and the number and arrangement of drawers within it can also be varied in many ways. Make a scale drawing before embarking on any project.

Bear in mind what the drawers will be expected to hold and make sure they are not so large that there is a danger of overloading them.

It is usual to have drawers lighter at the top, deepening to give a heavier, more solid appearance toward the bottom. Many modern designers dispense with this rule to make interesting patterned arrangements of the drawer fronts.

HANK WOLLER ● *Skyscraper cabinet*
This piece contains lots of interest, using natural wood and color for an effect which is enlivened by the textures and patterns of doors, drawers and cupboards. ▶

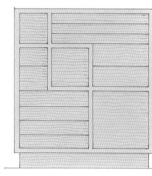

DRAWERS AND OPENINGS
Drawers can be combined with cabinet doors or arranged in an asymmetrical pattern.

Drawer runners
Drawers can be bottom-run, as in the chest of drawers in Module 4, or side-run. Side-run drawers have a blind groove routed out of the sides. This fits on a hardwood batten screwed and glued to the cabinet sides.

Readymade drawer slide systems are available in a variety of designs to suit anything from small lightweight drawers to deep, heavy kitchen drawers. If you use them, the drawer front must overlap the cabinet to cover the space needed for the slide system.

Tall narrow cabinet.

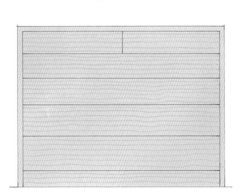

Combination of wide and narrow drawers.

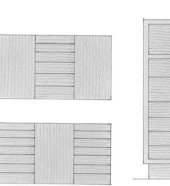

Symmetrical combination.

A modern asymmetrical style.

HANDLES

In addition to contributing to the appearance of the chest of drawers, handles must be easy to grasp and must be able to take the pull of a fully loaded drawer. You can make handles yourself, either as an integral part of the drawer front, or to attach, or you can choose from an almost infinite range of readymade handles.

Handle position

In classic furnituremaking, attached handles are never positioned on the center line of the drawer or door, but just above it. This applies whether the handle is placed at the edge, as on a cupboard door, or in the center. ▼

Handle position on a cupboard.

Handle position on a drawer.

Handle size

It is an important part of the design process to consider the size of handles and their relationship to the size of the drawer fronts. ▼

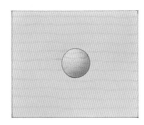

Consider handle size in proportion to drawer size.

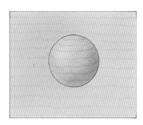

Large handles will dominate the design.

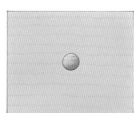

Tiny handles can make an interesting detail feature.

Style of handles

Handles can be routed or carved out of the solid wood of the drawer front. They can be a subtle addition to the design, or they can play a more dominant part in the design.

Handles made from dowels make a bold modern addition to the drawers. ▲

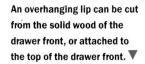

A purchased handle set at an angle adds an unusual touch. ▲

Rout out a recess for the handle in the drawer front. Insert a dowel or carved peg. ▲

An overhanging lip can be cut from the solid wood of the drawer front, or attached to the top of the drawer front. ▼

A grooved handle should be large enough for you to hook your fingers into. ▼

ROBERT INGHAM • *Chest of drawers*
This chest of drawers is an exquisite piece of furniture in its design, choice of material, detailing, and making. ◀

Chairs and Their Construction

The chair has always been a great challenge to designers, which is why there are so many variations on such a common object.

Chairmaking developed into a specialized craft from the simple frame systems. Mortise and tenon joints are still widely used in chair making, and much use is also made of dowels.

The chair became the most shaped and carved area of the furnituremaker's craft. An important element in chair design has been the development of upholstery. Designers, particularly in this century, have evolved many different ideas for the chair, both complex and simple forms and, in some, very advanced structures. The chair can often be furniture as art. Its styles often echo major movements in art, architecture, and design.

The back legs inserted at an angle

CHAIR CONSTRUCTION

While shaping has characterized the development of the chair, there are two common forms of normal chair construction: either make the two sides and join them together; or make the front and back and join these. The former generally happens with a complex arm and side shape, while the latter will generally be used when there is a complex back together with carved front legs.

Join the sides together

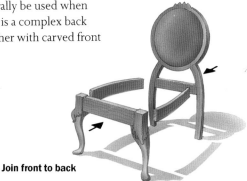

Join front to back

The "D" frame

As chairs developed shape, the old frame methods of construction were less appropriate, and the chair maker developed the "D" frame. The insertion of the back legs at an angle naturally gives a tapered back.

With the use of a steel band clamp and dowel joints between back and side rails and the back legs, the structure is glued into a very strong frame. It meant shapely chairs could be produced before the development of laminating or formed plastic shells. ▶

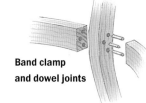

Band clamp and dowel joints

Victorian

Traditional chairs: Windsor chairs

These were traditional chairs made in the beech woods Europe where good wood was available. The design shown is quite a refined version. Country furniture also evolved the type of chair with turned legs and rails, often with a rush seat. ▼

Windsor chair

Traditional chairs: bentwood chairs

In a sense following the Windsor tradition, the firm of Thonet developed bentwood designs in Austria and produced a vast variety of different forms. The one shown in the illustration is one of the timeless classics, the café chair. It was one of the first items of mass production, 4 million being shipped in component (knock down) parts into America during the last decade of the 19th century. It has often been copied, but never equaled. ▼

Bentwood café chair

Modern chairs
Since the late 19th century, modern materials and manufacturing techniques have been fully exploited in chair design and manufacture.

After traditional Windsor and bentwood chairs, laminated forms were introduced, and later metals and plastics became widely used. These developments are often found more widely in the contract market rather than in household furniture. ▶

Laminated chair by Alvar Aalto

Steel wire chair by E. Race

Molded one-piece plastic chair by Verner Panton

During the periods of Art Nouveau and Art Deco, chairs became highly shaped and

There are many specialized chairs for specialized uses: two common ones are folding chairs and stacking chairs.

Folding chairs
A very traditional folding wooden chair folds from front to back. The other method is to fold from side to side. The chair by the Danish designer Mogens Koch is a lovely example of considered design.

Folding wooden chair

Folding wood and canvas chair

Stacking chair of laminated wood

Stacking chairs
Stacking chairs are generally made of metal or plastic, but the one shown here by Peter Danko uses laminated wood.

decorated. The illustration shows a chair designed around the beginning of this century by the Catalan architect Antoni Gaudi, of Barcelona, exemplifying the sculptural approach to the chairmaker's art. ▼

Art Nouveau chair designed by Antoni Gaudi

Molded plywood chair designed by Charles Eames

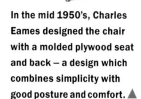

In the mid 1950's, Charles Eames designed the chair with a molded plywood seat and back – a design which combines simplicity with good posture and comfort. ▲

FURTHER **INFORMATION**	
110-117	Module 5: Upright chair
120-121	Upright chair
152-163	Module 8: easy chair
170-171	Easy chair

Upright Chair

Traditional chairmaking demands a high level of skill. The main challenge is that in order to fit the curves and angles of the human body, the components rarely meet at right angles. Modern chair designers tend to tackle this problem by combining straight sections with pre-curved components – as this design does.

This is the first project to introduce wood curving techniques. Curved seat and back pieces are attached to a straight-sectioned frame joined by mortise and tenon joints.

AIMS OF THE PROJECT
Introduce the techniques of shaping wood.

TOOLS YOU WILL NEED
Chalk
Pencil
Ruler
Panel saw
Marking gauge
Craft knife
Jack plane
Dovetail saw
Range of chisels
Mortise gauge
Try square
Power router or a rabbet or shoulder plane and a hand router
Spokeshave
Scraper plane
Bar clamps
Cabinet scraper
Sanding block
Screwdriver
Drill

TIME TO ALLOW
If you have made the previous projects, the underframe of this chair should take two or three weekends, depending on your power tools. Allow two weekends to make the seat and back.

REMEMBER
Plan your work schedule so that the correct sequence is followed.

HEALTH AND SAFETY
Follow the safe working procedures outlined on page 9.

CHOOSING WOOD

Beech, ash, and oak are often used in chairmaking, as a slightly flexible wood is needed. Beech is used specifically in upholstered chairs as it takes tacks and staples well without splitting. Your choice of wood for a single chair will depend on availability, and how and where you wish to use it.

No	Sawn	Planed
	CUTTING LIST	
2	BACK LEGS 2ft 4in x 1½in x 1½in	2ft 3in x 1¼in x 1¼in
2	FRONT LEGS 1ft 5in x 1½in x 1½in	1ft 3in x 1¼in x 1¼in
2	SIDE RAILS 1ft 6in x 3½in x 1in	1ft 5in x 3in x $^7/_8$in
3	CROSS RAILS 1ft 6in x 5in x 1in	1ft 4in x 4½in x $^7/_8$in 11in x 4½in x $^7/_8$in
	TO MAKE SEAT 1ft 4in x 3in x 1in	1ft 3in x 3in x $^3/_4$in
1	TOP BACK RAIL 1ft 3in x 1½in x 1½in	1ft 2½in x 1¼in x 1¼in
6	VERTICAL SLATS SAWN FROM SOLID 1ft 6in x 3in x 1¾in	Several can be sawn from 1 piece
1	CURVED TOP RAIL 1ft 3in x 3in x 1¾in	
+ glue, screws, masking tape, finishing		

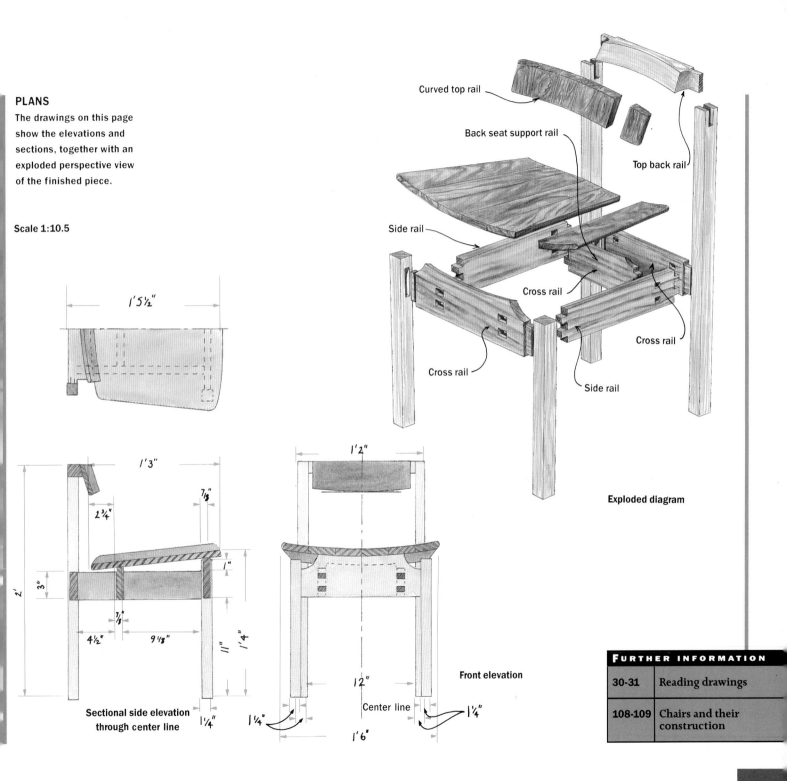

PLANS

The drawings on this page show the elevations and sections, together with an exploded perspective view of the finished piece.

Scale 1:10.5

Curved top rail

Back seat support rail

Top back rail

Side rail

Cross rail

Cross rail

Cross rail

Side rail

Exploded diagram

1' 5½"

1' 3"

7/8"

2¾"

1"

3"

2'

7/8"

4½"   9⅛"

11"   1' 4"

Sectional side elevation through center line

1¼"   1¼"

1' 2"

12"

Front elevation

Center line   1¼"

1¼"

1' 6"

BUYING WOOD

1 The wood is in two sizes, the legs being from 1½ inch material and the rails from 1 inch material. The seat and back barrel forms are from 1 inch thickness, but the top rail that holds the back is from 1½ inch thickness.

PLANE ALL COMPONENTS

2 Saw the components from the board, plane them all face side, face edge, width, and thickness, and leave slightly over length.

LAY OUT COMPONENTS

3 Lay out all the components, working from the face side and face edge and marking in pencil.

MAKING THE UNDERFRAME

4 Start with the frame before proceeding to work on the seat and back. Mark and cut the underframe components in the following order.

5 The two side rails and the back seat support rail are joined into an H-frame. The back seat support rail is wider than the side rails since it has to have the curve to support the seat cut into it. Mark the curve now, and the decorative curves at the side, and cut outside the line. True the main surface later when the underframe is glued, but smooth the curves with a spokeshave and scraper. ▼

6 The back seat support rail is joined to the side rails with twin through mortises and tenons. The twin tenon is a decorative feature and forms a stronger joint than a single large mortise and tenon. Mark them in pencil, check they are correct, mark with a scribe line, then saw and chisel the mortises and tenons.

7 Scrape all flat surfaces. ▶

8 Assemble the H-frame dry. ▶

9 It is convenient at this stage to drill holes in the back and front seat support rails for the countersunk screws that will later hold the seat in place. ▶

10 The front rail and back rail are also joined by twin through mortise and tenon joints to the two side rails of the H-frame.

11 The front rail has to have the curve formed for the seat. Mark the curve and cut outside the line as before. Leave precise finishing until later. Mark and cut the tenons that will fit into the legs on both the front rail and the back rail. Note that the shoulder lengths are not the same on the two rails.

12 Mark four sets of twin tenons on the side rails and their mortises on the front and back rails.

13 Assemble the H-frame and front and back rails dry. ▶

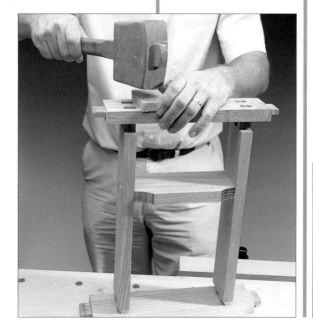

THE LEGS

14 Lay out the front legs and mark and cut the mortises. ▲

FURTHER INFORMATION	
24-25	Planing
44-46	Making a mortise and tenon joint
50-53	Advanced hand tools
164-165	Shaping wood

15 Dry fit the legs to the front rail. Repeat the process with the two back legs and back rail. ▲

16 Mark and cut the front legs and the bottoms of the back legs to length. Assemble all these components dry; you should now have an underframe that is together, but the back legs have nothing in between them at the top. ▼

CURVING THE SEAT SUPPORTS

17 Take a ruler, place it across the front rail and the back seat support rail, and mark the angle that you will need to spokeshave on the curved position of those two rails. ▼

ASSEMBLING THE FRAME

18 Even though the legs are now fitted to the frame, do not glue them at this stage. Sand the seat frame and glue this underframe assembly of five pieces together, starting with the initial H-frame and then adding the front and back rails. ▶

MAKING THE SEAT

19 The seat is composed of six slats glued together into a curved form. Prepare these pieces and mark the angles on the edges that will make the series of slats that form the curve.

20 Cut some scrap pieces of wood to the curve of the seat, then lay the slats on these and check that the angles when you plane are correct to form the required curve. It can help assembly if you make four of these curved pieces, two male and two female. A pair at the front and back help during clamping.

21 When the slats fit together dry, glue them. Put masking tape on the underside of the curve which holds the bottom edges together and run the glue on the two faces, allowing the masking tape to hinge them open. When you later rest the seat assembly on the female curve, all the joints close up.

22 Clamp across the barrel curve of the seat, and it is here that the male and female support curves are handy. C-clamp these lightly to the back and front of the seat and attach small bar clamps across the seat. You should get enough pressure to just squeeze those angled faces together.

23 Remove the glue before it has dried. When the glue has cured, take the seat curve out of the clamps and shape the seat. You can use a plane on the outside of the curve, but, you will have to use a spokeshave on the inside. ▼

24 Mark the taper on the seat from front to back and the slight curves on the front and on the back and saw to these lines. Plane the edges and shape the radii on the two sides. Sand the seat all over. ▲

25 Place the seat on the underframe sub-assembly. If necessary, adjust the curve on the front and back seat support rails. ▶

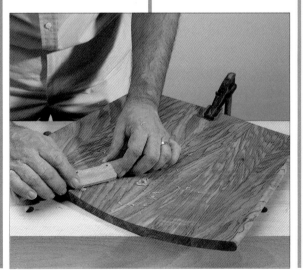

28 Cut and fit the lap joints, but do not glue in position yet. Cut the curve in the top back rail. Mark and cut the slats for the curved top rail. Since these slats will be glued into position, you do not have to make the barrel first, but can glue the slats to the curve of the top back rail. Place the center slat in position first and then place and glue the remaining slats. ▶

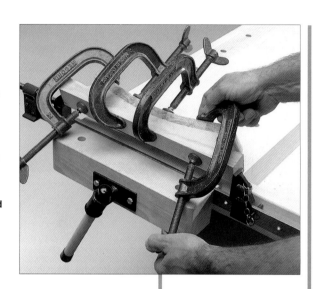

26 It is useful at this stage to position the seat and screw it into place. You may have to remove it before finally finishing the chair, but it is more manageable this way. ▲

MAKING THE BACK

27 The back legs are attached to the seat frame dry with a clamp holding them. Mark the top back rail with the lap joints that connect it to the top of the back legs, and mark the curve that will hold the slats that make up the back. ▶

29 Mark and cut the shapes on the bottom of the back rail and the radii on the sides of the back rest. ▶

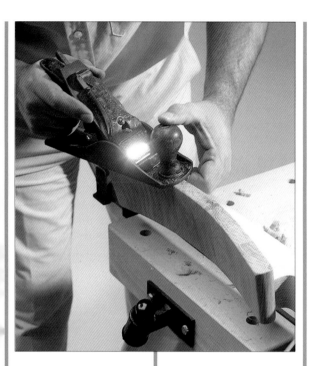

30 Plane the bottom of the slats and the top level with the top back rail. ▲

FINAL ASSEMBLY

31 Sand all the components. Glue the front legs to the front rail, the back legs to the back rail, and the back assembly to the top of the back legs. ▼

32 The finished chair. For a later project, you could make a set of these chairs. ▼

FURTHER INFORMATION	
24-25	Planing
70	Holding and clamping
164-165	Shaping wood

Dowel Joints

Doweling is a traditional technique and is widely used in the craft of chair making. Dowels were sometimes also used in traditional woodwork as pins to hold a mortise and tenon joint.

Dowels can be used for joining chipboard and other manmade boards.

Dowels

For a well-made joint, the dowel must fit tightly in the hole and a minimum of ¾ inch of dowel should extend into each piece. The combined depth of the holes should be slightly greater than the dowel length.

You can buy dowels in different diameters and lengths ready-made for joining. These have grooves cut in the sides to allow air and excess glue to escape from the hole as the joint is clamped. The dowel ends are chamfered to allow them to go more easily into the holes.

MAKING YOUR OWN DOWELS

It is quite simple and economical to buy a length of dowel rod and cut it into the number of dowels needed for joining. You are most likely to need dowels of ¼, ⅜ and ½ inch diameter.

1 Cut the dowels to length as and when you need them. ▲

2 Use the marking gauge to cut grooves in the dowel to allow air and glue to escape when the joint is clamped up. ▲

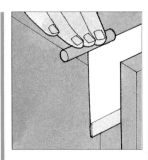

3 Alternatively, clamp a tenon saw upside down in the bench vice and run the dowels over the teeth to groove them. ▲

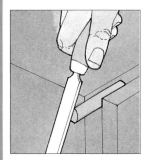

4 Chamfer both ends of the dowels for easy entry into the drilled holes. Use a rasp, or buy a dowel pointer, which is rather like a pencil sharpener, turned in a brace or drill while the dowel is held upright in the vice. ▲

LAYING OUT

Like all joints, doweling relies on precise layout. You can buy jigs to help with layout and drilling, but it is possible to achieve a good match very simply.

Faces to be marked must be flat and square. A minimum of two dowels are necessary for each joint. Larger or heavier work may call for more dowels.

Make sure that the shoulders are flat and square, and mark the positions on one component using a square, gauge, and knife.

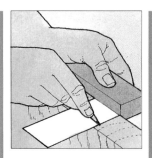

1 With the wood held securely in the vice, use the square to mark the dowel centers. Mark from the face side. ▲

2 Set the marking gauge to half the rail thickness, and mark across the centers from the face side. ▲

TRANSFERRING MARKS

1 Use brads to transfer marks from one component of the joint to the other. Mark the hole centers on the first piece of wood and drive a brad into each one. ▶

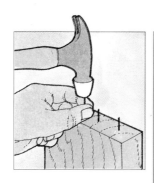

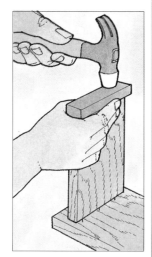

2 Cut the heads off the brads with pliers or cutters. Then align the second piece and press or tap it down to locate the hole centers. Remove the brads with pliers. ▶

3 Center points are made specifically for marking dowel joints. Mark and drill the holes in the first piece of wood. Insert the center points and press the second piece into position to transfer the marks. ▶

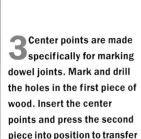

DRILLING

Once the centers of the holes have been laid out, drill the holes using either a brace and bit, a hand drill, or a power drill.

1 Use a brad-point drill bit to locate precisely in the hole centers you have marked. A twist drill bit is liable to wander from the center. ▲

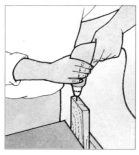

2 It is essential to drill square to the surface and not at an angle. Stand in line with the wood to make sure you are drilling parallel to the sides. Use a depth stop to make sure you drill to the required depth (see right). ▲

DEPTH STOPS

Wood must often be drilled to a specific depth, for example, when making dowel joints or to ensure the drill does not break out on the other side of the wood. You can buy a depth stop to fit around the drill bit, or wind a piece of tape around the drill at the required depth.

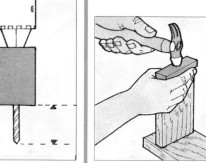

Making your own depth stop

Make sure the drill is firmly located in the drill chuck. Decide on the depth of hole and mark that distance on the drill from its end.

Measure from the mark to the chuck and make the stop from a piece of wood the same length. Drill a hole through the wood the exact diameter of the drill bit. Smooth off the sharp edges to prevent damage to the work, and fit it over the bit. ▲

ASSEMBLING THE JOINT

1 Check that the dowel joint is correctly aligned with a dry run, before applying glue. ▲

2 Add the glue to the holes, not the dowels, to prevent the dowels swelling. Use a mallet, or a hammer protected with a piece of waste wood, to tap the joint components together. ▲

Upright Chair

The chair is one of the most challenging items for any furniture designer. An upright chair must be strong enough to withstand many different stresses, yet be light enough to be pulled up to a table or desk.

Many of the traditional solutions to problems posed by chairmaking remain the best, but there are still plenty of opportunities for design variations.

A chair is judged on comfort, and this is not due to the amount of upholstery it has, but to the angles and positions of the individual parts of the chair and the support the frame gives to the body. In a well-designed chair, body muscles don't have to work to maintain a comfortable posture.

HANS WEGNER • *Chair*
With a seat of woven cane, the flowing back and arms of this chair make it a classic of its kind. Originally designed in 1947, this chair is another example (see right) of Danish mass-produced articles based on the tradition of hand-crafted work. ◄

SUPPORTING THE BODY

In an upright or "working" chair, the body needs support in five places: under the heels, under the pelvic bones, and in the lumbar region, or small of the back.

Center of gravity

The best position for accomplishing tasks, whether eating, writing, or typing, is one where the spine is upright with the center of gravity running down the backbone from the skull to the pelvis.

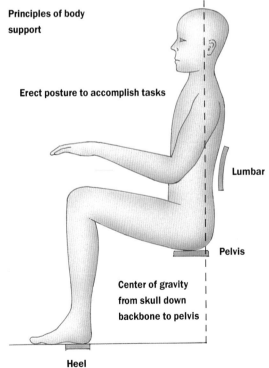

Principles of body support

Erect posture to accomplish tasks

Lumbar

Pelvis

Center of gravity from skull down backbone to pelvis

Heel

Basic position

This basic position is maintained whether the person is seated cross-legged on the floor, or in the "Balans" position proposed by Norwegian researchers in the 1980s. In this position, the body weight is shared between the pelvis and the knees. ▼

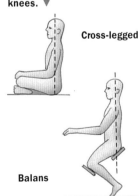

Cross-legged

Balans

Chair sizes

Optimum chair sizes to suit the average adult have developed over time, and designers now have a set of dimensions from which they can begin work.

These basic measurements are the starting point for a wide range of design adaptations. The measurements must be adapted to suit anyone who is not of average height and build.

If you are designing a chair to match a table, make sure that the chair will be able to be pulled up to the table. ▶

h = seat height
15½ to 17 inches
Always start working from this measurement. If the

HANS WEGNER • *China chair*
Hans Wegner has been one of the most prolific and consistent of the Scandinavian designers. Throughout his career he has produced classic, timeless pieces that are still fresh today, 40 years after they were designed. ◀

chair is too high, it presses into the backs of the thighs; if it is too low, it may be difficult to get out of.

p=pelvic support
6 inches
This is the area which supports the weight of the body.

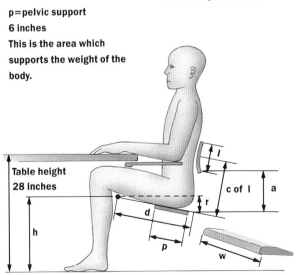

d=seat depth
13½ to 15 inches
A chair that is too deep presses on the backs of the legs, while one that is too shallow may be unstable.

r=seat rake
approximately 1 inch or 5 to 8 degrees. The seat is angled down from the horizontal to support the natural tilt of the pelvis and the lumbar curve of the spine. Working and desk chairs are often flat, which makes it easier for the user to lean forward to type or write.

c of l = center of lumbar
8 inches
The distance from the rear of the seat to the center of the lumbar area where back support is needed.

l=lumbar region
4 inches
This is the area that should be shaped to follow the lumbar

curve. For a high back, extend this area at an angle of 20 to 25 degrees to the vertical to support the shoulders.

a=arm height from rear of seat
9½ inches
Use this dimension to calculate the height of an arm rest, or the relative height of a table top.

w=width of seat
19 to 20 inches between arms
   Seat width often tapers from front to back to allow room for legs at the front while leaving clearance for elbows at the rear.

JOHN MAKEPEACE WORKSHOPS • *Phoenix chair*
A very dramatic design. Made with a laminated holly bark, with burr elm, bleached and scorched oak, it has a positive presence. The choice of materials greatly enhances the qualities of the chair. ▲

FURTHER INFORMATION	
108-109	Chairs and their construction
110-117	Module 5: upright chair

4 Advanced Course

These final projects apply and develop in different ways the skills you have learned earlier. The desk has drawers, uses mortise and tenon joints, and introduces new carcass construction techniques – frames with panels. You can easily customize the desk design to suit your own requirements. With the fine boxes, your woodworking moves onto a different plane. The solid wood box develops craftsmanship with the incorporation of through dovetails. The plywood boxes give an opportunity to experiment with varieties and colors of veneer. Finally, the easy chair is a major project, but by now you should not find it difficult, since it applies previous knowledge.

Desk

This desk brings together a number of the techniques you have learned and practiced in earlier projects.

Making this project demonstrates how a complicated furniture construction is broken down into a series of simpler components – frames, carcasses, drawers, and framed panels. Each component is made separately, then combined in stages into the completed desk.

CHOOSING WOOD

With the experience gained on earlier projects, you should be able to choose any quality hardwood that is available and that fits in with your decor.

CUTTING LIST		
No & Part	**No & Type**	**Sawn**
1 TOP	2 long rails	3ft 2in x 2¼in x 1¼in
	2 short rails	1ft 10in x 2¼in x 1¼in
	1 sheet	3ft x 1ft 8in x ½in plywood or MDF
2 SIDE FRAMES	4 legs	2ft 6in x 1¾in x 1¼in
	4 rails	1ft 9in x 2¼in x 1¼in
1 REAR FRAME	2 long rails	3ft x 2¼in x 1¼in
	2 short rails	1ft 8in x 1¾in x 1¼in
	1 sheet	2ft 9in x 1ft 4in x ⅜in plywood or MDF
1 DRAWER FRAME	4 cross rails	3ft x 3 @ 2¼in
		1 @ 3¼in x 1in
	3 side rails	1ft 8in x 5½in x 1in
	8 drawer runners	1ft 8in x 1½in x 1in
2 DRAWERS	2 drawer fronts	1ft 5in x 5½in x 1¼in
	4 drawer sides	1ft 7in x 4in x ¾in
	2 drawer backs	1ft 5in x 3in x ⅝in
	2 drawer bottoms	1ft 5in x 12in x ¼in plywood or MDF

PLANS

The drawings on this page and overleaf show the elevations and sections, together with an exploded perspective view of the finished piece.

Scale 1:10

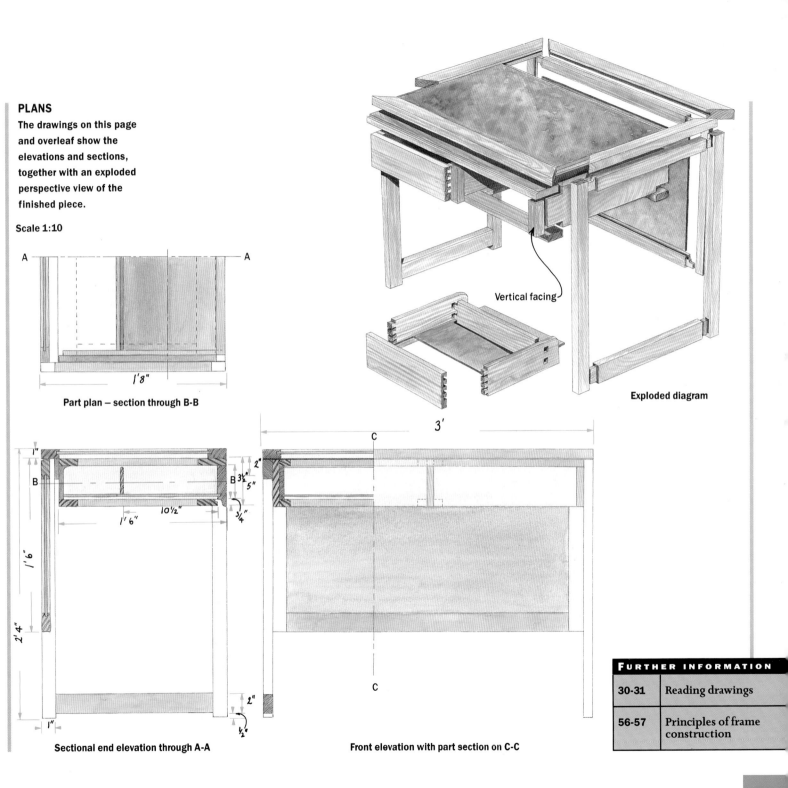

Part plan – section through B-B

Vertical facing

Exploded diagram

Sectional end elevation through A-A

Front elevation with part section on C-C

BUYING WOOD

1 Most of the solid wood is bought sawn at 1¼ inches to finish at 1 inch. The drawer unit and drawers use 1 inch or ¾ inch to finish at ¾ inch and ⅝ inch. You also need three pieces of plywood or MDF.

2 Mark and saw out all components. Then plane them and leave slightly over length.

3 The project is designed in the form of a set of components, so the process for each one is described in order.

SIDE FRAMES – MAKE TWO

4 Mark mortise and tenon joints on the four legs and four rails. The rails should have shoulders all around and the top rails a haunch.

5 Cut and fit the joints. Assemble the frames dry, check that they are both the same size and that they are square and flat. Disassemble and sand all the components.▼

6 Reassemble, glue, and clamp. Afterward, give a sanding and a coat of finish.

SURFACE FINISH – TOP AND REAR FRAME

7 These finishes should be considered before you make up the panels, and at the same time since they will be seen together.

Linoleum was used for the prototype, since it gives a pleasant writing surface. You can buy plywood or MDF that is pre-veneered if you wish to save time. You could also apply your own veneer, use plastic laminate, or paint the surface. Whichever you choose, the finish should be applied before either panel is inserted in the frame.

REAR FRAME – MAKE ONE

8 This is a frame and panel. Mark the vertical stiles and the horizontal rails for the frame and cut the groove on the inside faces that will take the panel.

9 Mark and cut all mortise and tenon joints. Remember that the haunches will fill the groove.

10 Assemble the frame dry and mark the plywood panel to be a snug fit in the frame. Cut and fit the panel.

11 Disassemble the dry frame, check that the panel fits and everything is square and flat. Glue and clamp it together. When the glue has cured, sand and apply final finish. ▲

TOP – MAKE ONE

12 Cut the frame material to slightly over the finished size. The panel has a rabbet cut around the edges to fit into grooves in the frame.

13 Mark the four pieces for the frame edging, cut the grooves around the inside edges. Mark the panel precisely to its final size, and cut the rabbet around all four edges. ▼

14 Begin to apply the four frame pieces to the panel. Care is needed, since the frame corners will be mitered and you are building this frame around the panel. Cut the miter on the long sides and dry clamp them to the board. Then fit the short ends so that the frame is tight around the panel and the four miters are a good fit. ▼

15 Glue and clamp the frame to the panel. After the glue has cured, sand and finish the frame. Set the top aside with the side frames and the rear frame. ▶

DRAWER FRAME – MAKE ONE

16 Mark all components. The two side pieces have the cross rails attached to them. The upper front cross rail is wider than the other three since the drawer front sits underneath flush with its edge.

17 Due to the grain direction on the sides, it is not good practice to dovetail these four rails, so the four corners are notched. ▲

18 The cross rails are screwed and glued in place. ▼

19 Rather than see end grain on the front of the side rails, add a small edge banding at the front. ▼

FURTHER INFORMATION	
44-46	Making a mortise and tenon joint
47	Preparing the surface
60-61	Finishes
70	Holding and clamping

20 In the center of the frame, a small vertical partition runs from front to back to separate the two drawers. It is notched to the front and back rails, and screwed in place like the ends. This frame is not difficult to make, but it is essential to lay out very precisely so that the places where the drawers will run are square and parallel. ▲

21 Add the drawer runners, eight in all. These are attached by screws in between the four long cross rails and provide a surface on which the drawers slide and run. This component can now be sanded and finished. ▼

DRAWERS – MAKE TWO

22 These are made in a similar fashion to previous drawers. Notice that the drawer sides are the complete depth of the drawer frame, but the back is located in one-third from the back edge. Drawers should only be pulled out two-thirds of their possible length; if you pull them right out, they and their contents can end up on the floor.

23 Plane the drawer sides to be a smooth-running fit. Make sure that the back fits the opening precisely. Fit the front. Make grooves in the sides and the front to take the plywood bottom. Gauge the thickness of the side on the ends of the back and front. Make twin through tenons between the back and sides and half-blind dovetails between the front and the sides.

24 Assemble the drawers and fit them in the frame. They should now run smoothly in the drawer frame. ▲

25 Form the drawer handles from routed grooves underneath the drawer fronts, or by cutting spaces in the lower front rail. ▼

OVERALL ASSEMBLY

26 Attach the side frames to the end of the drawer frame and the end of the rear frame. The desk can be assembled permanently using dowels, biscuits, or splines or by screwing the side frames to the desk frame and rear frame.

The prototype was screwed. The advantage of using screws is that if you customize the desk to make it larger, it is much easier to transport the components and assemble them in the room.

27 Screw the side frames at the top from the inside of the drawer frame. ▶

28 The easiest way to screw the rear frame in position is from the outside of the side frames into the end of the drawer frame and the end of the rear frame. The screw heads are then visible in the side frames. Recess the screw heads into a hole and plug that hole if you wish to hide the screws. However, many woodworkers find Posidrive or Allen-head screws are visually quite acceptable. ▶

29 When the basic structure has been assembled, place the top in position and attach it with screws from underneath. Complete the final finish to all components. Slide the drawers into position. ▶

30 The finished desk brings together earlier woodworking techniques and some new ones. ▲

Machine Planing

Only hand planing can give you a real "feel" for wood. It is important to master the skill of hand planing first, since it is the only way to understand how the blade cuts, how different woods and grain directions affect the finish. This feeling is absent in machine planing, but machines do remove the hard drudgery of larger jobs.

ELECTRIC HAND PLANE

This tool cuts with knives held in a revolving cutter head. It is essential to make sure that all guards are properly attached and that safe procedures are used to make sure that your fingers and hands cannot come near the revolving head.

When you plane an edge with a hand plane, it is often a help to use your leading hand as a guide, holding the side and bottom of the plane. *Never* do this with an electric plane.

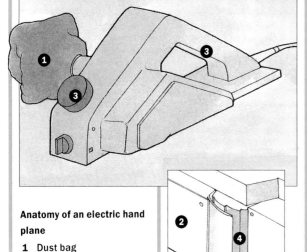

Anatomy of an electric hand plane

1 Dust bag
2 Sole
3 Handles
4 Cutter head with planer knives

You can buy a useful attachment to hold the plane with the planing face up to convert it into a jointer. Note the procedures outlined below for using jointers. Always follow the manufacturer's instructions on the use of guards.

1 When planing along the grain, keep your hands on both handles. Set the plane to make shallow cuts, and plane slowly for a smooth finish. ▲

JOINTER

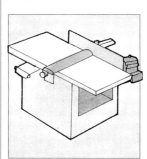

The jointer enables you to plane a surface, a square edge, or an angled edge. Never attempt to plane short material; work should always be 12 inches or longer. ▲

2 If the work is twisted, make passes across the grain. Always make finishing cuts along the grain. ▲

Planing the face side

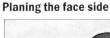

1 It is important to take the correct stance, standing beside the jointer, just behind the cutter head. ▲

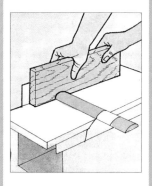

2 The jointer has guards that ensure you cannot get your hands near the cutter head, either a bridge guard, or one that pivots out of the way when the work is over the head. Always use these guards. ▲

3 Feed the wood from the lower infeed table toward the cutter head, which is set slightly higher. The outfeed table is the same height as the cutter head knives. Depth of cut is adjusted by raising or lowering the infeed table. ▶

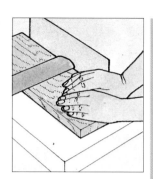

4 When feeding the wood, which may have some twist in it, put pressure first on the wood on the infeed table. ▶

5 When the knives have started to cut, and the wood has emerged from under the guard, move your leading hand, and then the other hand, to ensure the wood lies flat on the outfeed table. This movement becomes second nature with practice. ▶

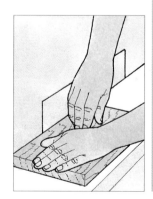

Planing an edge

Check first that the fence is square with the table. Make sure all guards are in place, and feed the wood, using the same sequence of movements as planing the face, but this time also make sure that the face side is flat against the fence. ▼

Planing an angle

1 To plane an angle other than 90°, adjust the angle of the fence. Take extra care to make sure that the face side is pressed against the fence. ▼

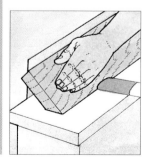

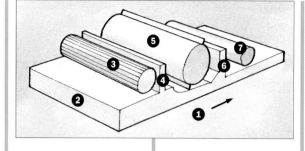

Anatomy of a thickness planer

1 Direction of wood feed
2 Wood to be thicknessed
3 Infeed roller
4 Infeed pressure bar
5 Rotating cutter head
6 Outfeed pressure bar
7 Outfeed roller

THICKNESS PLANER

1 Once the jointer has smoothed the face side and the face edge, the thickness planer ensures that the work is accurately planed to the required width and then to thickness. ▲

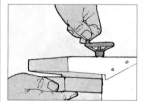

2 Do not attempt to take too deep a cut. When feeding the wood in, always keep your fingers away from the infeed rollers. ▲

3 To plane thin wood, use a base board. You can easily make one from scrap wood. Screw an end batten onto the board to keep it in place. Feed the thin pieces along this false platform. Do not attempt to plane thin wood to width. ▼

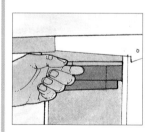

Desks

A desk needs a writing surface at a comfortable height and normally includes some form of storage for writing implements and stationery.

Nowadays, desks must accommodate computers and peripheral equipment of varying shapes and sizes. The home office also needs filing and other document storage.

Simple desk

The desk is a writing table with one or more drawers. The table surface can be inlaid with some resilient material that feels pleasant to write on. The table top may be flat, or simple storage can be placed along the back. ▶

Pedestal desk

A pedestal or kneehole desk takes the writing table one step further with frame and panel sides to create storage areas in one or both sides. ▶

"Partner's desk"

The traditional "partner's desk" is a large, solid and imposing version of the pedestal desk, framed all around. ▶

ANDREW LAWTON • *Chevron desk*

A lovely, restrained design with elegant details. The folded panel ends make the most of some lovely figured wood and the wedged-through tenons are well-placed. A fine piece of drawer making with interesting handles, complemented by a subtly colored top. ▶

JUDITH AMES • *Desk (and chair)*

The table is a simple four-leg design, enriched by curves on the legs and on the rails. The contrast between the woods works well, and the whole has a classic, timeless look that will last. ▼

Writing desk

The writing desk developed in the 17th century. The sloping fall front opens to create the writing surface and to reveal a variety of pigeonholes and storage compartments. When open, the front is supported by pull-out lopers. The basic idea can be developed with arrangements of drawers or cupboards below and a bookcase on top. ▲

Brass hinges

Brass hinges are the alternative means of supporting the fall front. The internal storage is set back slightly to allow for the movement of the hinge. Hinges may also be curved, or cranked with a hinge in the middle. ▶

Roll-tops

The roll-top desk became popular in the U.S. in the 19th century. The tambour, or sliding door, is made of wooden slats glued to a canvas backing. This flexibility means the tambour can slide around curves. ◀

Workstations

With computers, the desk has become a "workstation" that must provide space for a variety of different pieces of equipment. Keyboards should be placed 2 inches lower than a writing surface to avoid strain, while the monitor may be placed higher, at eye level. ▲

DAVID DELTHONY • *Clam desk*
A very interesting sculptural form, with surfaces on two levels, the upper for writing, the lower for keyboard use, both deriving from one folded form. The desk is approached from three sides, one for writing, one for typing, and the third for access to the storage drawers. The form of the top, and the shapes of the pedestal, complement each other. ▲

Veneers

Veneers are thin slices of wood, used for decorative or constructional purposes. Wood is converted into decorative veneer because some species are too rare or expensive to be used as solid wood, or their structure makes them unsuitable to be used in solid form. When glued to a stable substrate, they produce fine colors, shapes, patterns, and textures that may be impossible to achieve using solid wood.

Do not think of veneer as a substitute, or as giving a lower-quality result. Veneer is a viable and respectable alternative to solid wood.

Decorative veneers are usually quite thin $1/64$ to $1/32$ inch thick. Constructional veneers are used in the production of plywood or laminated shapes and are generally much thicker, from $3/32$ to $1/8$ inch.

VENEER PRODUCTION

The specialized veneer manufacturer must be able to gauge the likelihood of valuable or interesting veneer that will result from cutting by looking at the uncut log. The expertise of the veneer cutter lies in knowing how to cut the log to produce the greatest quantity of valuable veneer. It is possible to cut large sheets from some wood, but in wood with unusual features, the veneer sheets will be quite small. There are three main methods of cutting veneer: rotary cut, sliced, and sawn.

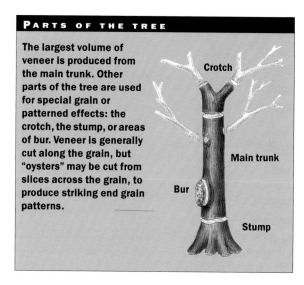

PARTS OF THE TREE

The largest volume of veneer is produced from the main trunk. Other parts of the tree are used for special grain or patterned effects: the crotch, the stump, or areas of bur. Veneer is generally cut along the grain, but "oysters" may be cut from slices across the grain, to produce striking end grain patterns.

Crotch

Main trunk

Bur

Stump

Saw cutting

Before the development of veneer slicing machines in the eighteenth century, all veneers were cut by sawing. Now sawing is only used for particular species or logs that are difficult to peel or slice, or where a particular grain feature can be obtained only by sawing.

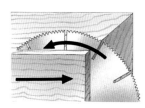

Saw cutting is very wasteful. Up to 50 percent of the log may be lost in the saw cut. ▲

Rotary cutting

The log is first softened by soaking in water or steaming. A large knife is set to cut the veneer to the required thickness, assisted by a pressure bar which helps the veneer part evenly.

The log is held between centers, and rotated against the knife to produce a continuous sheet of veneer.

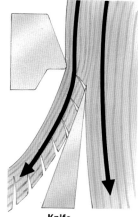

Knife

The knife is set in front of the pressure bar by the required thickness of the veneer. ▲

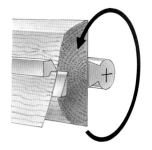

Veneer cut from a half-round log is narrower, but has a similar figure to veneer produced by off-center cutting. ▲

This is an efficient method for producing large sheets for plywood and laminates; it is also used for some decorative veneers, particularly to produce the bird's-eye effect in maple.

Rotary cutting produces veneer with a distinctive pattern produced by the tangential cut through the growth rings.

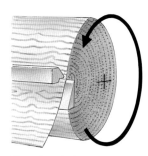

Mounting the log off-center produces a wide veneer, but with a decorative grain figure. ▲

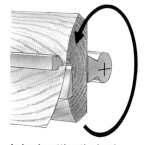

In back cutting the log is mounted with heartwood facing outward to produce decorative figures such as burs and curls. ▲

Slicing

This method produces decorative hardwood veneers. The log is first cut lengthwise, and its grain is assessed to determine how further cuts can produce the most interesting or valuable veneers.

The log is further cut into "flitches" which are mounted on a sliding frame. As the frame moves down, it pushes the wood against the knife blade and pressure bar to slice off a sheet of veneer.

The flitch can be mounted in several different ways to produce various grain patterns.

Flat-sliced veneer may also be cut tangentially from a quartered log; this produces narrow but attractive veneers. ▲

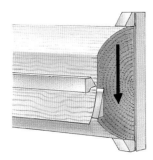

Flat slicing is the most common method and produces traditional crown-cut veneer with bold curves and ovals. ▲

TYPES OF VENEER

Decorative veneers are always cut to maximize the attractive features of the wood species.

Veneers are stacked in sequence from the slicer so that patterns can be matched, and they are then sold in sequence. To match veneers, always take them consecutively from the pack.

Veneer can be commercially colored, subtly or in vivid hues; lines, bandings, and readymade patterns are also available.

Stringing lines are fine strips used to divide different areas of veneer.

Decorative bandings are made from side grain sections glued together and then sliced into strips. Always buy enough of each pattern to complete a project, as you may not be able to obtain the exact color and pattern again.

Inlay motifs are bought readymade to inset in a veneer surface or for use in marquetry. If possible, the inlay should be the same thickness as the veneer for even pressure during gluing. Traditionally, other materials like mother-of-pearl and brass have also been used for veneer inlay.

Veneers, inlays and bandings
1 Aspen
2 Colored pine
3 Tropical olive
4 Olive ash
5 Brazilian rosewood
6 Cherry
7 Zebrano
8 Pomelle
9 A selection of different inlay motifs
10 Patterned bandings and stringings

FURTHER INFORMATION	
146–147	Veneering
166–169	Bending and laminating

Fine Boxes

Precision marking and cutting are more important than ever when making small objects because our eyes are drawn to look closely at joints, the way things are put together, and the detailing.

The first box is made in solid wood and has through dovetailing as a structural and visual feature. The second box is veneered and relies for its effect on the choice of veneer.

AIMS OF THE PROJECT
To produce the finest quality work and make detailed decorative dovetails.

TOOLS YOU WILL NEED
Chalk
Pencil
Ruler
Panel saw
Marking gauge
Craft knife
Jack plane
Block plane
Dovetail saw
Coping saw
Small chisels
Mortise gauge
Try square
Power router, or a rabbet plane or shoulder plane and a hand router
Nail set
Bar clamps
Cabinet scraper
Sanding block

TIME TO ALLOW
The solid box will take two to three weekends; the veneered box could be done over a series of evenings, probably about 1½ weeks in total.

REMEMBER
Leave the four sides in one strip and the top and bottom in one strip when you are planing the sawn boards to size.

HEALTH AND SAFETY
Follow the safe working procedures outlined on page 9.

CHOOSING WOOD

Only a small quantity is needed for the solid box, so choose an exciting and exotic wood. The prototype is made out of yew because, although it is difficult to work, it has a lovely appearance.

The veneered box is constructed from plywood. Again, not much material is needed, so you can choose some really interesting veneers that have patterns on a suitable scale.

No	Sawn	Planed
C U T T I N G L I S T : S O L I D W O O D B O X		
TO CUT AND MAKE 4 SIDES, 2 LONG & 2 SHORT		
1	2ft 2in x 3½in x ¾in	2 @ 7in x 3in x ½in 2 @ 5in x 3in x ½in
1	TO MAKE TOP 7in x 5in x ¾in	6½in x 4½in x ⅝in
1	TO MAKE BOTTOM 7in x 5in x ½in	6½in x 4½in x ⅜in
+ masking tape, glue, finishing, veneer pins, hinges (optional)		

No	Sawn	Planed
C U T T I N G L I S T : V E N E E R E D B O X		
TO CUT 4 SIDES		
1 plywood	12½in × 4¾in × ⅜in	After wood strip set in to plywood at top/bottom division line
1 solid wood	12½in × ½in × ⅜in	4 @ 3in × 5in × ⅜in
TO MAKE TOP AND BOTTOM		
2 plywood	3⅛in × 3⅛in × ⅜in	3in × 3in × ⅜in
FOR INSIDE AND OUTSIDE		
2 sheets veneer, not less than 19in × 6in × ¹⁄₃₂in		

PLANS

The drawings on this page and overleaf show the elevations and sections, together with an exploded perspective view of the finished piece.

Scale 1:3

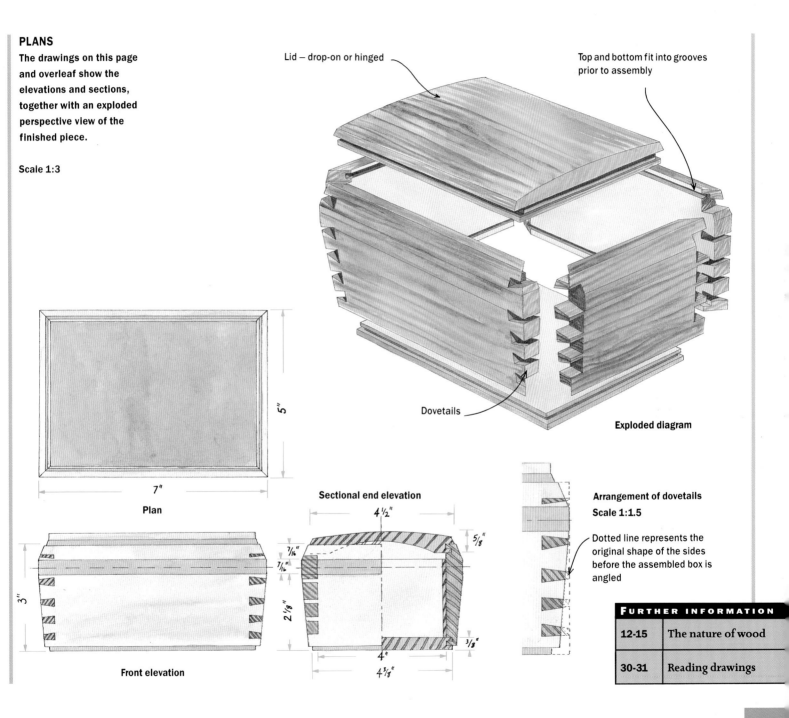

Lid – drop-on or hinged

Top and bottom fit into grooves prior to assembly

Dovetails

Exploded diagram

5"

7"

Plan

Front elevation

3"

Sectional end elevation

4½"

5/8"

7/16"

7/16"

2⅛"

4"

4⅝"

3/8"

Arrangement of dovetails
Scale 1:1.5

Dotted line represents the original shape of the sides before the assembled box is angled

FURTHER INFORMATION	
12-15	The nature of wood
30-31	Reading drawings

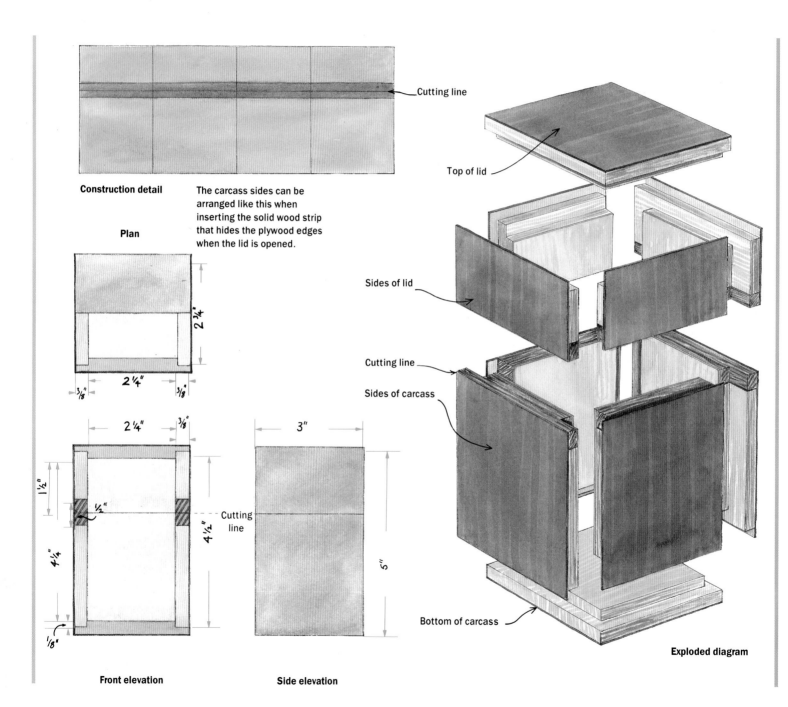

Construction detail

The carcass sides can be arranged like this when inserting the solid wood strip that hides the plywood edges when the lid is opened.

Cutting line

Plan

2¾"

2¼"

³⁄₈" ³⁄₈"

Front elevation

2¼" ³⁄₈"

1½"

½"

4¼"

4½"

Cutting line

¹⁄₈"

Side elevation

3"

5"

Cutting line

Top of lid

Sides of lid

Cutting line

Sides of carcass

Bottom of carcass

Exploded diagram

SOLID DOVETAILED BOX

1 Mark the components on the wood and saw them. Plane all components and cut them slightly over length.

JOINING THE SIDES

2 Work out the size and proportions of the dovetails on the four corners. The prototype has dovetails which diminish in size from one edge to the other, but you could choose any pattern. The box is constructed square, and the sides planed at an angle afterward.

3 Make scribe lines around the shoulders and the ends. Make a pencil line $1/16$ inch outside the scribe lines and saw the sides to that length.

4 The bottom and top of the box have miters. These miters allow the grooves that hold the top and bottom to be cut without showing at the corners, the miter covering the grooves. Check your layout, then cut the grooves.

MARKING AND CUTTING DOVETAILS

5 Cut the pins first and mark the tails from them. On the two short sides that are to receive the pins, very carefully mark the dovetails on the end grain, pencil in the parts that will be waste, and put a scribe line and gauge line across the end and down the sides to the shoulder line. ▼

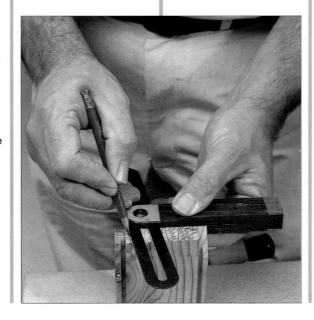

6 Cut the pins, sawing down the waste side of the line to the shoulder line in each case. Saw out the waste with a coping saw. ▼

7 Carefully pare the shoulders. Do this on each of the four corners. ▶

8 With the long sides on the bench, the inside face uppermost, position the cut pins and mark the tails from them. It may be worth using a clamp to ensure that the pieces do not move. ▲

9 Mark the waste with a pencil and cut to the waste side of the lines you have just marked with a dovetail saw and then cut out the waste with a coping saw. Pare to the shoulder lines.

10 You cannot try the joints dry until you have cut the miter, two on each corner. Mark the miters with a scribe line and saw about $^1/_{16}$ inch away from this line so that you can tap the joint together and fit each corner, paring where necessary.

11 When the joints are fitted and it looks as if they will go together well, finally cut the miters. You should now have four sides to the box, joined by the dovetails, but dry without glue. ▲

MAKING THE TOP AND BOTTOM

12 Cut the top and bottom precisely, remembering to allow for the overlap and the splines that will fit in the grooves on the box sides. Lay out accurately and plane the bottom and top to size. Cut the grooves that will allow them to fit into the grooves in the sides.

13 The box top has a curved face; shape that now. Also make the bevel on the top sides and, if you wish, the internal carving on the inside of the lid. It is not essential, but is often done with small boxes to lessen the weight of the top. ▲

14 Disassemble the four sides and check the fit of all parts. Sand and finish all inside surfaces, making sure you mask the joint surfaces of the dovetails. You can, however, finish the grooves in the sides and top and bottom, since the construction here allows for a slight movement of the wood in the top and bottom in the frame. ▼

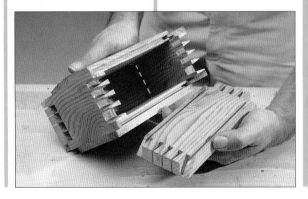

15 Glue the joints and assemble the box, removing from the clamps when the glue has cured. Plane the outsides from their original rectangular shape; this gives the box some interest, especially in the apparent reduction in the size of the dovetails.

16 Gauge a line around the completed box where you wish the lid to separate from the bottom. ▼

17 Saw the top from the bottom. ▲

18 Plane the joining surface so that the top fits the bottom exactly. ▼

MAKING THE BOX LININGS

19 Linings fit inside the box and are mitered at the corners. They need careful planing since they should be as tight as possible without allowing them to bow. Finally, finish the box. ▼

20 The prototype is made with a simple drop-on top, but if you wish you can install hinges.

21 The finished box, sealed and waxed to bring out the grain. ▶

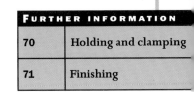

VENEERED PLYWOOD BOX

1 Purchase your veneer and some ³⁄₈ inch plywood. Lay out and cut the components. You should have two squares for the top and bottom and one piece from which four sides will later be cut.

2 When you cut the lid from the bottom, that cut will expose plywood on the joint faces. The box will look much better if, when it is opened, only solid wood is visible. So, before you do any work on the joints, make a cut approximately where you wish the lid to separate on the piece that represents the four sides and glue in a strip of wood. ▲

3 You can make the insert slightly thicker than the plywood but make sure that the plywood is perfectly flat when re-glued. When the glue has cured, plane the insert down so that the piece is flat again.

4 Cut the four side pieces. You now need to apply the inside veneer to these sides and the two top/bottoms. This small job can be easily accomplished by pressing the plywood and veneer between two blocks. Always put waxed paper between the outside face of the veneer and the block.

5 When the glue has cured, remove from the clamps, trim the veneer, sand and finish the inside surfaces. ▲

6 Carefully cut the six pieces to the exact size and join them using a very simple lap joint. Check that the box goes together dry. Glue the corner faces. ▼

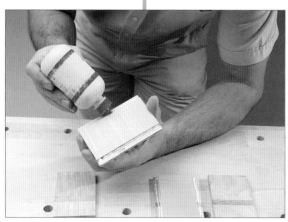

7 Bring the four sides together and use veneer pins to assemble the box. Be careful that the pins do not go through the inside face. It is useful, with the pins holding the parts in position, to clamp the four pieces in the vice or in a C-clamp to ensure a tight fit. ▲

8 Check that the four-sided box is square. ▶

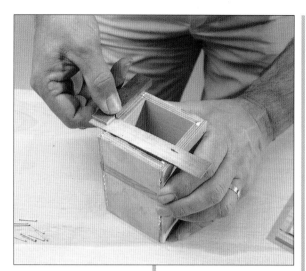

9 Before gluing on the top and bottom, remove the excess glue from inside the box. ▶

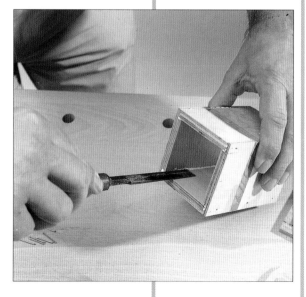

10 Glue and pin the top and bottom to complete a six-sided box. You will not be able to remove the glue from the inside of the top and bottom until later, but because the inside surfaces have been finished, this should not be difficult. ▼

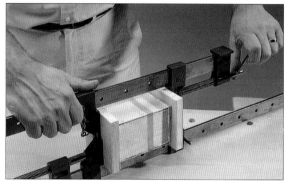

11 Punch the heads of the pins below the ply surface. ▶

FURTHER INFORMATION	
134-135	Veneers
146-147	Veneering

12 Plane the six outside faces, ensuring that each is flat and parallel with its opposite side. ▼

13 Mark with a large "T" which of the two ends is the top surface because otherwise you will not know where the wood insert is located when you cut the top from bottom. Make sure you have a diagram or pattern which tells you exactly where this insert is.

14 Apply veneers to the outsides. First take two of the opposite rectangular faces and apply the veneer. ▼

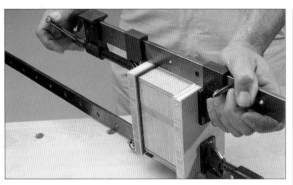

15 Clamp the box. Use scrap wood as protective blocks to protect the veneered surface during clamping. ▲

16 When these veneers have cured, very carefully trim the veneer all around, paying special attention to the four long edges.

17 Repeat the process so that all four sides are veneered. Trim again. ▶

18 Mark with a scribe line where you will separate top and bottom since, as soon as you apply the end veneer, you will lose your "T" mark. Glue the veneer to the top and bottom. Trim the veneer very carefully, sand all over and apply the first finishing coat.

19 Re-mark the position of the lid and cut the lid from the bottom. ▼

20 Carefully plane the finished rim so both sides fit. ▲

21 The lid is located in position by dowels at the four corners. First mark the position of the dowels in the lid. ▼

22 Using pins transfer these marks to the box bottom. Drill and install top dowels, and drill corresponding holes in the bottom. ▼

23 Check all over and apply final finish. ▲

24 The finished box, finished to a rich glow. ▼

FURTHER INFORMATION	
24-25	Planing
26-27	Sawing
71	Finishing
146-147	Veneering

Veneering

One of the thrills of woodworking is to use solid wood. However, some wood is too expensive or has grain that is unsuitable to work in solid form. Many exotic woods are available only as veneer.

In industry, veneers are applied in a hydraulic press with heated platens. Traditional woodworkers make a hand press or "caul" to do a similar job. The technique described here shows how to apply and press veneer with a simple handmade caul.

Veneer can also be applied by hand using animal glue, pressing the veneer with a special veneer hammer. This is a very skilled technique and is usually limited to restoration or reproduction.

APPLYING EDGE BANDINGS

Edge bandings are generally applied to manufactured board that is to be veneered, and can be solid wood or veneer. They can be attached in a variety of ways: glue only; tongue and groove; spline or biscuit.

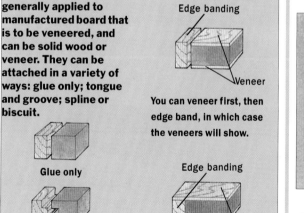

Edge banding

Veneer

You can veneer first, then edge band, in which case the veneers will show.

Edge banding

Veneer

Or you can edge band the board first and finally apply veneer.

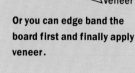

Glue only

Tongue and groove

Spline or biscuit

APPLYING AND PRESSING

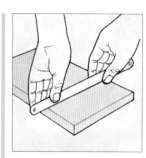

1 Careful preparation is necessary. The substrate or face on which the veneer is going to be applied should be flat and clean. You can roughen the surface slightly with a saw blade to provide a key for the glue. ▲

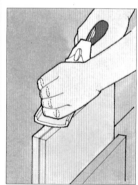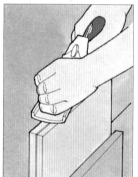

2 If joining is needed to make the sheets of veneer wide enough, the joint must be precise. Clamp the veneer between two boards and plane the edges straight. ▲

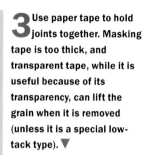

3 Use paper tape to hold joints together. Masking tape is too thick, and transparent tape, while it is useful because of its transparency, can lift the grain when it is removed (unless it is a special low-tack type). ▼

4 The veneer must be cut slightly oversize, about ½ inch extra all around, so mark this cutting line on the veneer using a pencil. ▼

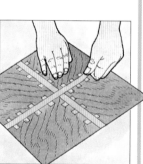

5 Cut veneer with a sharp craft knife against a steel straightedge. Cut about ⅛ inch outside the pencil line, and cut across the grain first as this is most likely to split. ▲

6 If pieces of veneer must be cut and joined, do this first, then apply to the substrate in one piece. ▲

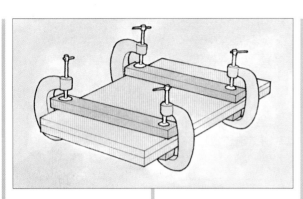

10 Apply the veneer, smoothing it down by hand. Then with a clean roller, press it down, working from the center to the edges. The principle with veneering is always to squeeze glue from the center outward and make sure that no air is trapped. ▼

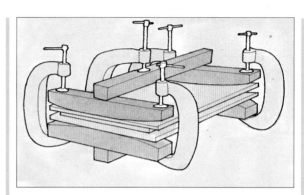

7 Make the caul or press from two large boards or sheets of particle board, chipboard or MDF at least ³/₄ inch thick and larger than the panel to be veneered. Do not use joined boards for the caul. ▲

9 The choice of glue is important. Use either white glue or urea formaldehyde (plastic resin) glue. It is not generally advisable to use contact cement for veneer. Only use it when applying surfaces like plastic laminates or linoleum. Metal surfaces, tiles, and mosaics need special adhesives.

Apply glue to the substrate only and not to the veneer. It is worth spreading the glue with a roller to obtain a film of consistent thickness. ▼

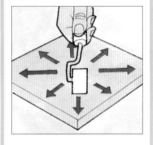

11 Large C-clamps will give enough pressure on a small job. But because of the depth of throat on most C-clamps, there will not be enough pressure on the center of the caul. ▼

12 On a larger job, use battens, cut to a slight curve, on the outside of the caul. Then when the clamps are tightened, pressure is applied first to the center of the caul. ▲

13 Allow enough time for the glue to have thoroughly cured before opening the press.

The time will depend on the type of glue used, but overnight is always preferable, except if you are using hardeners or accelerators to part-cure the glue. Keep the workshop at a reasonable temperature, 60-70°.

Trim the veneer with a sharp craft knife, remove any paper

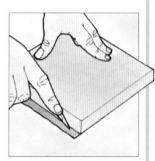

tape with a little warm water, and then sand lightly before applying a finish. ▲

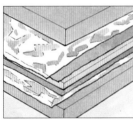

8 It is a good idea to finish and wax the inside surfaces of the caul. With some veneers, the glue can seep through and may stick to the caul. For the same reason, always place paper or clean waxed paper between the caul and the veneer. ▲

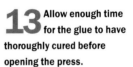

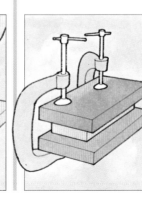

Hinging

A wide choice of hinges is available to the woodworker. Most work needs good-quality hinges, the best being solid brass butt hinges. The technique illustrated here shows the procedure for attaching hinges to a box, but the same principles apply to hanging doors.

First decide where to place the hinges on the edge of the box. Arrange them not too near the end, but in a position about equal to the hinge length from the corner. Three or more hinges may be necessary for larger boxes or chests.

Types of hinge

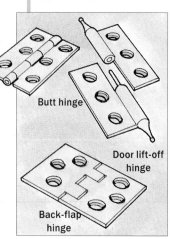

Butt hinge

Door lift-off hinge

Back-flap hinge

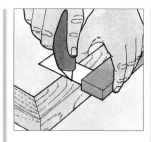

FITTING HINGES

1 Measure from the end and make a knife mark at this position on either the top or bottom of the box. Then carefully mark the hinge length from the hinge itself. ▲

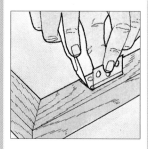

2 The center of the hinge pin should be positioned exactly at the corner edge of the bottom and top. Your marking must place the hinge in this exact position. ▲

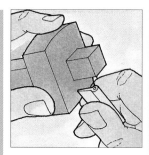

3 From the first knife location marks, square cut lines on the closing face and outside edge. ▼

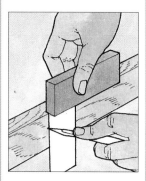

4 Then with the two parts held together, transfer these marks to the other part. Make an approximate pencil mark to prevent the cut lines from going too far down the outside of the box. ▼

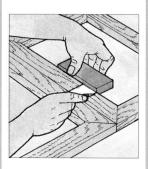

5 Set your marking gauge to the exact width of the hinge, measuring from the inside edge of the hinge to the center of the hinge pin. ▲

6 Gauge the hinge widths from the outside edges on the closing faces of both top and bottom. ▲

7 Re-set the gauge to the thickness of the hinge from its face to the center of the pin and gauge these lines from the closing faces on the outside edge of the box top and bottom. ▼

8 Notice that the thickness of the hinge at the edge is smaller than the distance from the face to the pin center. The section you will remove to set the hinge into must be slightly sloped. ▼

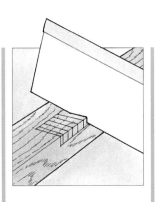

9 To remove most of the waste wood, carefully saw a series of cuts at an angle between the two gauge lines. ▲

10 Carefully chop a series of chisel cuts across the grain from the gauge line at the rear of the closing face to a depth on the inside hinge edge equal to the thickness of the hinge. ▲

11 Carefully pare the waste. You should now have a recess into which the hinge fits very snugly and which should be a perfect match on the top and bottom. ▼

12 Place the hinge in position in the recess and mark the exact center of one of the screw holes, drill a pilot hole, and insert one steel screw. ▼

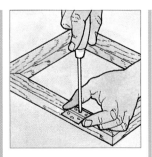

13 Attach both the hinges to the lid first. Then you should be able to mark, drill, and screw the hinge in position to the bottom part using only one screw in each hinge leaf. ▲

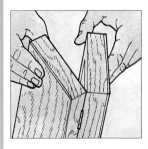

14 You can now check that the lid closes properly, and if you need to make any slight adjustments, screw holes that have not been marked yet will enable you to re-position easily. Drill the pilot holes for the remaining screws. ▲

15 Remove the hinges and plane a slight chamfer on the sharp hinge edges of the box. This ensures the lid can swing freely. ▶

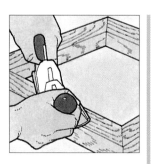

16 Insert all the brass screws into the hinges on the lid first. The final appearance is always improved by aligning the screw slots in one direction. On very fine work, polish the brass hinges with very fine sandpaper followed with brass polish.

When using brass hinges, you need brass screws, but never insert a brass screw initially. Always insert a steel screw of the same gauge and length first, remove it, and insert the brass screw. This is because brass is softer than steel, and in difficult and hard wood it is easy to break the screw head. Always lubricate screws, but especially brass ones, with petroleum jelly, wax, candle wax, or soap. ▶

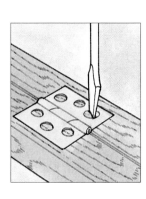

Boxes

Boxes and other small items give you an opportunity to explore the use of many different and exotic woods that may be too scarce or expensive to use for larger pieces.

Work at this scale needs very careful consideration of scale and proportion. Always make full-size drawings of any project. For unusual shapes, it is worth making a model in cardboard.

Your work will be handled and studied closely, so think very carefully about any structural and decorative details that you wish to add.

MAKING SOLID WOOD BOXES

Solid wood boxes can be made in any size. The interior can be fitted with a set of removable trays and fixed or movable compartments.

The box top can drop on, or it can be hinged in different ways, and have a range of locks and catches attached. Buy good-quality hardware for your work, even though they may be expensive. Cheap, poorly made hardware can be troublesome and spoil the look of an otherwise beautiful piece of work. Solid or extruded brass hardware is superior to folded or pressed brass.

Make the corner joints a feature of the work by using decorative through dovetails. They can be given added emphasis by combining different woods in a single box. The proportion and arrangement of the pins and tails is a matter of individual choice. Full-size working drawings will help you to plan the joints.

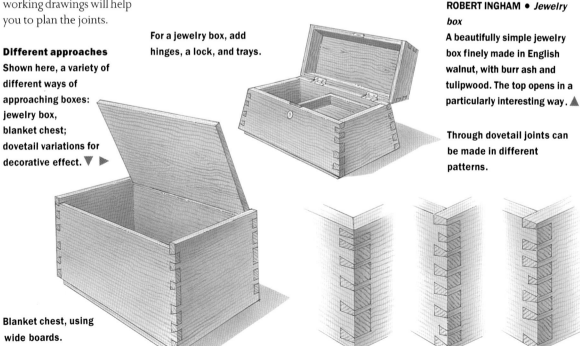

Different approaches
Shown here, a variety of different ways of approaching boxes: jewelry box, blanket chest; dovetail variations for decorative effect. ▼ ▶

For a jewelry box, add hinges, a lock, and trays.

Blanket chest, using wide boards.

ROBERT INGHAM ● *Jewelry box*
A beautifully simple jewelry box finely made in English walnut, with burr ash and tulipwood. The top opens in a particularly interesting way. ▲

Through dovetail joints can be made in different patterns.

ANDREW WHATELEY • *Display case*
The shell concept was arrived at by considering how to display and store a set of antique spoons. The fit between the two halves and the hinging mechanism show precision woodworking, and the shaping and finishing is exquisitely achieved. ▲

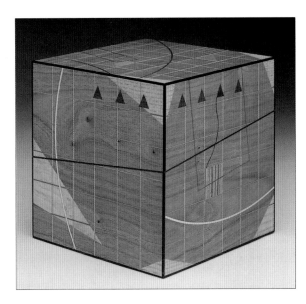

NIC PRYKE • *Veneered box*
A very interesting veneered box which demonstrates skill in making and imagination in conception and development.

PLYWOOD BOXES

Plywood boxes joined with simple lap joints can be any shape you choose. The material is stable, relatively inexpensive, and quick to cut with power tools – the limits are only your time and imagination.

Using lap joints means the construction method is hidden, so boxes of this kind are ideal for experimenting and developing your skills and finishes and veneers. In addition to exotic wood veneers, there are manmade and colored veneers. You could also use decorative bandings and inlays.

Consider each box as a complete shape; quickly made cardboard models will often give you a better idea of the likely success of a design than a drawing.

Use laminating and bending techniques to introduce curves and even circles.

Rectangular shape

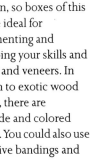

Square shape

Polygonal shape

Vary the proportions of polygons.

Triangular and tapering shapes.

Pyramid

Use veneers or laminates to create curves.

Lightweight veneers can be bent around in one.

Laminates or heavier veneers need making in two halves, either circular or elliptical.

A decorative tongue and groove joint makes a feature of the joint.

Use bending and laminating techniques to make sculptural boxes.

FURTHER INFORMATION

| 136-145 | Module 7: fine boxes |

Easy Chair

This chair calls for two different shaping techniques: shaping curved rails from solid wood, and making curved slats from laminate strips. You can buy veneer for the laminate, or cut your own.

The chair is comfortable as it is, but can also have a seat cushion made of leather or fabric filled with feathers.

AIMS OF THE PROJECT
To learn about shaping and laminating.

TOOLS YOU WILL NEED
Chalk
Pencil
Ruler
Steel ruler at least
2 feet long
Panel saw
Bowsaw, jigsaw, or bandsaw
Marking gauge
Craft knife
Try square
Jack plane
Mortise gauge
Dovetail saw
Set of chisels
Spokeshave
Rasps
Rifflers for shaping arms
Power router or a rabbet plane or shoulder plane and a hand router
Bar clamps
Cabinet scraper
Sanding block
Screwdriver
Drill

TIME TO ALLOW
Allow at least four or five weekends.

REMEMBER
When laminating, make sure that each piece is kept in the form long enough for the glue to cure fully.
Marking curves is difficult to do single-handed. You will need to call on a helper briefly for step 11.

HEALTH AND SAFETY
Follow the safe working procedures outlined on page 9.

CHOOSING THE WOOD

The design calls for "sturdy" looking wood. Wood with too fine a grain would be less appropriate than woods like oak, ash, teak, beech, or elm. The prototype was made in cherry. Your choice may be affected by the material for the laminated back slats. If you buy veneer, your choice will be limited by the species available, but if you intend to cut and plane your own veneer, there will be no such limitation.

No	Sawn	Planed
CUTTING LIST		
2	BACK LEGS 2ft 9in x 2in x 2in	2ft 7in x 1¾in x 1¾in
2	FRONT LEGS 1ft 10in x 2in x 2in	1ft 8in x 1¾in x 1¾in
3	CURVED CROSS RAILS 2ft x 3in full x 2½in	1ft 10½in x 3in x 1¼ on curve
2	SIDE RAILS AND 2 ARMS 2ft 3in x 3in full x 1¼in	2ft 2in x 3in x 1in
7	SEAT SLATS 1ft 9in x 2¼in x ¾in	1ft 8½in x 2in x ⅝in
6	BACK SLATS 2ft 6in x 2in x ½in	

Each to be laminated from 8 veneers 2ft 6in x 2in x 1/16in total of 48 required.

+ For laminating form: softwood approx 2ft 6in x 6in x 2½in; large sheet of paper, or graph paper, for full-size drawing of back slats; waxed paper; screws; glue

PLANS

The drawings on this page and overleaf show the elevations and sections, together with an exploded perspective view of the finished piece.

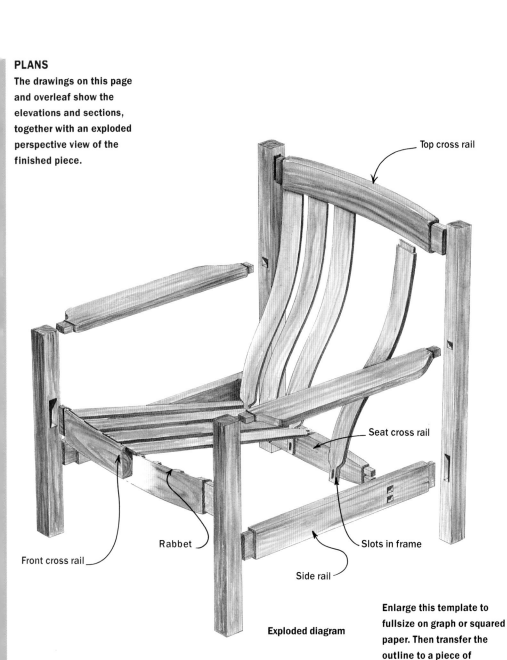

Top cross rail

Seat cross rail

Rabbet

Slots in frame

Front cross rail

Side rail

Exploded diagram

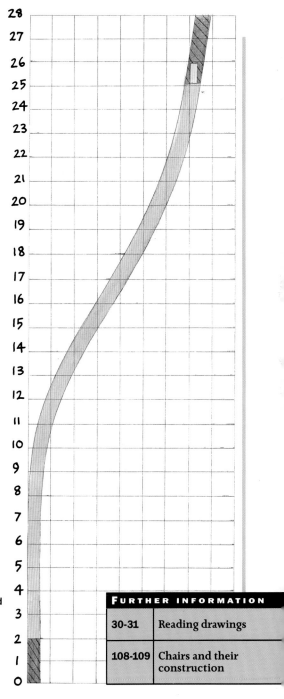

Enlarge this template to fullsize on graph or squared paper. Then transfer the outline to a piece of softwood to make the lamination former. Each square equals 1in.

FURTHER INFORMATION	
30-31	Reading drawings
108-109	Chairs and their construction

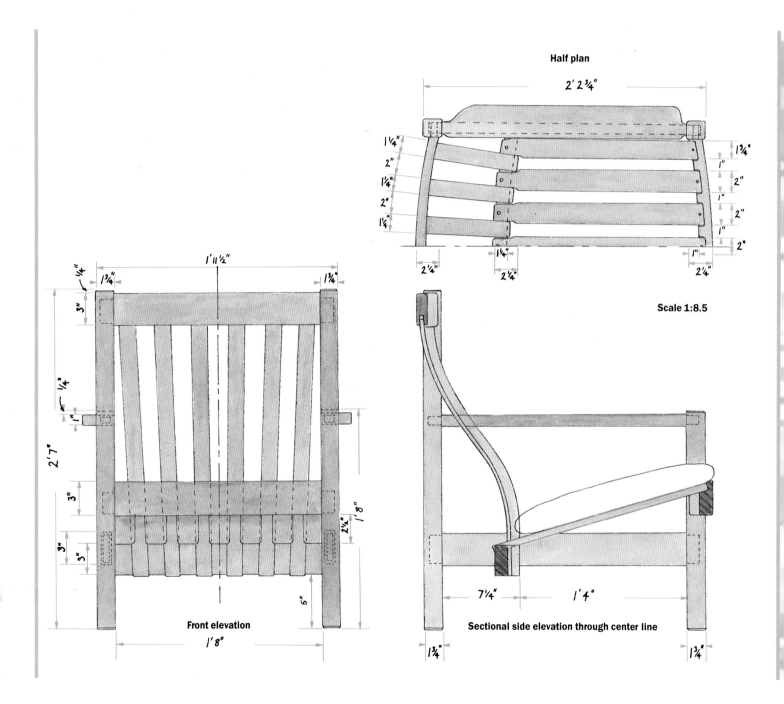

Half plan

2' 2¾"

1¼"
2"
1¼"
2"
1¼"

1¾"
1"
2"
1"
2"
1"
2"

2¼"
2¼"
2¼"

1¼"
1"

Scale 1:8.5

1' 11½"

¼"
1¾"
1¾"

3"

¼"

1"

2'7"

3"

3"
3"

2½"
1'8"

5"

Front elevation

1'8"

7¼"
1'4"

Sectional side elevation through center line

1¾"
1¾"

1 Prepare all wood except back slats to face side, face edge, width, and thickness.

3 Mark the tenons on the end of the cross rails, side rails, and the arms. The tenons on the side rail have shoulders all around. Mark the through mortises on the side rail, that will accept the twin through tenons on the seat cross rail. These through mortises run with the grain for strength. The seat cross rail is set low in the side rail.

5 Cut the mortise and tenon joints for the two side frames. Also cut the mortises for the cross rails. When cutting through mortises, mark and cut from both sides. ▲

SHAPE THE ARMS

6 Each arm is set so that the inside face is in line with the inside surfaces of the legs and the outside edge protrudes. To begin shaping the end, drill a hole to make the inner curve at the end of the arm and saw into the hole.

SIDE FRAMES

2 Mark the lengths of the legs. Mark the positions of the mortises for the side rails, the arms, and the mortises that will take the top and front cross rails. All mortises into the legs are blind mortises. ▲

4 Check the marking and make scribe lines and gauge lines where you intend to cut. Remember that you are making a matching pair of frames, right and left.

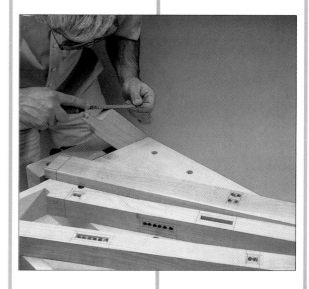

7 Finish the shape with rasps, files, and sandpaper. You can be more adventurous with this shaping if you wish. ▲

FURTHER INFORMATION	
44-45	Making a mortise and tenon joint
164-165	Shaping wood

DRY ASSEMBLY

8 Assemble both frames dry and check that the frames are square and not twisted and that the joints are tight. Then disassemble and sand the four sides of the arm and side rail and the two inside surfaces of each leg. ▼

GLUE, CLAMP, AND FINISH

9 Glue up both frames, clamp and remove excess glue. When the glue has cured, remove from clamps, sand and apply a coat of finish, ensuring that you mask the faces of the joints where the cross rails will be attached.

THREE CROSS RAILS

10 These rails should be planed all around, but will be oversize on thickness to allow for cutting the curves on the front and back. Mark the rails to length, both sides and tenon lengths.

11 Draw the curves with a pencil. It is sufficient to bend a steel ruler between the two end points and the center mark. It helps to have a partner to hold the ruler on the center mark and pencil the line. ▶

12 Trim the ends of all three rails to the overall rail thickness and pencil mark the tenons. ▼

13 Saw the curve. If you only have hand tools, use a bowsaw or a coping saw, but this is a slow process. Alternatively use a power jigsaw or a bandsaw. ▶

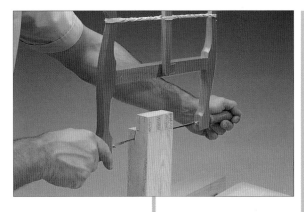

14 The three rails have a planed surface top and bottom, square ends marked ready for the tenons, and a sawn curve on the outside and inside faces. The curved surfaces must now be completed. Clean up the outside curve with a plane, except at the ends near the tenons, which will have to be pared. Smooth the inside curve with a spokeshave.

MARK AND CUT JOINTS IN THE CURVED RAILS

15 The top cross rail has a simple tenon on each end that fits into the mortise on the top of the back legs. Mark the mortises on the underside of this rail to accept the six back slats. Mark, check, and cut these joints. ▶

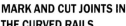

16 The front cross rail has two simple tenons that fit into the front leg. Mark and cut the tenons now. Later this rail will need a bevel at the top edge, which is best marked when the whole frame is assembled dry. It will also need to have recesses cut to receive the seat slats, but this is best done after the slats have been located into their fanned position.

17 The seat cross rail has twin through tenons that fit into the side rails. The shoulders on these tenons are longer than on the other two rails. The underside of this rail sits partly below the side rail, and the tenons are made near the top of the seat cross rail to allow for this. Mark and cut these tenons.

18 Make all the above joints, number or letter them, sand the rails, and assemble the whole frame dry. ▼

19 With a ruler placed between the seat cross rail and the front cross rail, measure how much bevel is needed on the front rail. Mark with a pencil, remove the front cross rail, and cut the bevel with a plane. Reassemble.

LAMINATED BACK SLATS

20 Make the form from a scrap piece of wood. Enlarge the drawing of the back slats to full size. Do this with graph paper or by making a grid of squares and plotting the points where the lines of the curve cross. Transfer this shape to the center of the form, and cut the shape with a bowsaw, jigsaw, or bandsaw. Clean up the faces.

VENEERS

21 If you purchase these, aim for a thickness of between $1/16$ inch and $1/8$ inch. The number you need for each laminated slat will depend on this thickness since the slat will have a finished thickness of $1/2$ inch. Each veneer strip should be 33 × 2 $1/4$ inches wide. Cut the strips with a craft knife against a steel ruler. ▼

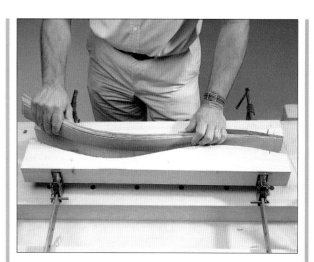

22 Alternatively, if you have the machines, you can make your own veneers. Plane a piece of wood 33 inches long x 2$1/4$ inches thick x a convenient width. Cut a strip off the side planed face 2$1/4$ x $1/8$ inch plus. Reface the sawn side on the piece and cut another strip. Repeat refacing and cutting until you have the number of strips needed. They will have one face and two edges planed and one face sawn. Use the thickness planer to plane the strips to $1/8$ inch thickness. Make a baseboard to support the thin strips safely.

23 If your veneers are $1/8$ inch thick, you need four to make each slat. Try these dry in the form to check that when clamped they are pressed closely together and, if necessary, adapt the mold faces. ▲

APPLY GLUE TO THE VENEERS

24 The glue needs to be capable of holding laminates, so either use urea formaldehyde, or one of the stronger formulated white or yellow glues. Apply the glue to all internal surfaces, not the two outer outside ones, and ensure coverage by using a glue roller. ▶

LAMINATES IN JIG

25 Wrap the glued bundle of laminates in waxed paper so that they do not stick to the mold when the glue squeezes out. ▼

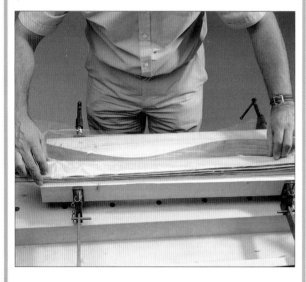

26 Place the bundle in the mold and tighten the bar clamps. Try to make sure that the veneers stay in line. The less neat the package, the more you will have to trim off and the result might not be wide enough for your needs. ▶

27 To ensure an even pressure, you will need five clamps, three on the underside and two placed on the top of the form after the first squeeze. ▶

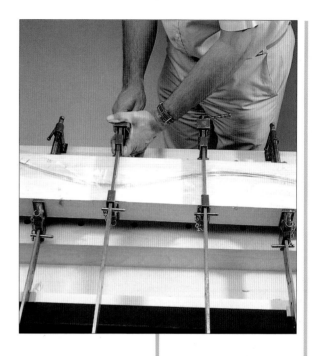

28 When the glue has cured (make sure you allow enough time for this), remove from the form. This is a process that you could do each evening during the week, since it is only possible to make one laminate at a time in the one form, and it should cure overnight. ▶

FURTHER INFORMATION	
70	Holding and clamping

29 Plane one of the laminate edges, using the form as a support. ▲

30 Alternatively, hold the laminate in the vice. ▼

31 Gauge the laminate strip to width. ▲

32 Saw to the gauged line and plane the last edge. The laminate is now ready for fitting into the frame. ▼

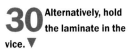

FITTING BACK SLATS INTO THE FRAME

33 Make the tenons on the top of the back slats to fit into the mortises cut in the underside of the top cross rail (step 15).

Mark the top shoulder line of each tenon from the form. If you do not make sure that the line is marked on each slat in the correct place at the correct end, the curves will not line up when assembled.

Clamp the slats together to mark the tenons. Cut the tenons. The shoulder lines are not yet at the correct angle; you will mark and cut this when you place each slat in its fanned position on the chair frame. ▲

34 Push the tenoned slats into the mortises on the top rail. ▼

35 Mark the center line on the seat cross rail. ▼

36 Take the two center back slats, and place them in their fanned position on the seat cross rail. When you are happy with this position, mark it in pencil and hold the slats in place with two C-clamps. ▼

37 Now mark each tenon shoulder line at the top of the slat with a craft knife. Remove each slat from the frame, pare the tenon shoulder accurately to the scribe line. The two slats can now be pushed home into the mortises.

38 The bottoms of the slats are narrowed where they are screwed to the seat cross rail. This is to allow the seat slats to fit between them. Mark the narrow part on the two center back slats. Take the seat slat that will fit between them, and mark the narrow point on it as well. ▼

39 To get the curved edge on the narrow part, start with a drilled hole, then saw, and finish the curve with a spokeshave. ▼

FURTHER INFORMATION	
24-25	Planing
44-46	Making a mortise and tenon joint
70	Holding and clamping
164-165	Shaping wood

41 Continue fitting the rest of the back slats: mark the position on the seat cross rail, mark and cut the tenon shoulders. Fit the tenons, narrow the ends of the slats, drill screw slots, and screw in place. Notice the mortise and tenons are not yet glued.

40 Drill screw holes. If you cut slots for the screws instead of holes, they will allow for any slight movement when sitting in the chair and will relieve the top tenons of any stress. ▼

FIT SEAT SLATS

42 Starting with the center slat, narrow the slat where it will be screwed to the seat cross rail. Narrow the other slats and place in the fan position. Mark the recesses for them on the front rail. ▶

43 Remove the rail again from the frame and cut the recesses. This can be done either by hand with saw and chisels, or with a router.

44 Replace the front rail in the frame and finally fit the seat slats. You will find that, due to the curvature of the seat and front rails, the rear of the slats will not sit flat. Cut the angle to allow each slat to fit. Drill the hole and insert the screw. ▶

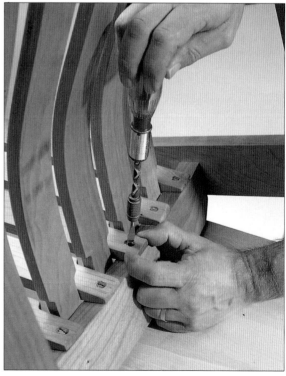

45 Mark the length of the slat and trim if necessary to ensure that it seats snugly in the recess on the front rail. Drill the front hole and screw into place. Repeat with the other slats. ▶

FINAL ASSEMBLY

46 Remove all screws, slats, etc., and sand all components (but do not remove your identification numbering).

47 Assemble the main seat frame, apply glue to the joints on the three cross rails, and clamp the frame. Remember to check for squareness and remove surplus glue. ▶

48 When the glue has cured, remove clamps and final sand. Finish the frame, but mask the mortises on the top back rail.

49 Mask the tenons on the top of the back slats, and sand and finish all the slats.

50 Install the back slats, applying glue and light clamping pressure to pull the mortises and tenons together. Screw the slats at the bottom, then remove clamps. Then screw the seat slats into place.

51 Finally, check the finish. Apply a coat of wax polish if required.

52 The finished easy chair; elegant and comfortable. ▼

FURTHER INFORMATION	
70	Holding and clamping
71	Finishing

Shaping Wood

Much woodworking is based on the square or linear approach used in cabinetmaking. Making curves and free shapes in solid wood call for different techniques and can be a very satisfying aspect of woodwork.

The techniques introduced here are often used in chairmaking, and as an example, they are shown being used to produce a cabriole leg, a style found in antique and reproduction chairs and tables. The same techniques are also used in much freer shaping for wood carving and sculpture.

Detailed drawings are essential. For more complicated shapes, make a rough model or prototype from some easily shaped material like balsa wood, styrofoam or plaster of Paris so that you can see the form from all angles and be sure you are achieving the shape you want.

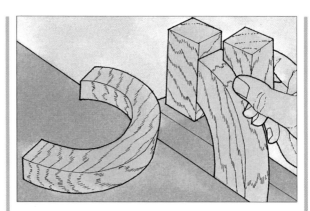

CUTTING CURVES

Curves are imposed on wood grain and do not always follow it. Where a curve results in "short grain," the wood will be weaker and more liable to break than where the length of the grain is used. Always bear this in mind when planning a project. You may need to attach an extra piece of wood with glue, screws, or dowels to overcome the problem. ▲

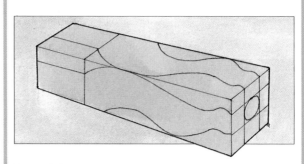

SAWING COMPLEX COMPONENTS

1 The cabriole leg is complex in shape, especially when seen in three dimensions. Initial drawing and planning are the all-important first steps. Draw the shape out on one face, then on the second and on the ends. ▲

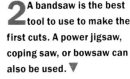

2 A bandsaw is the best tool to use to make the first cuts. A power jigsaw, coping saw, or bowsaw can also be used. ▼

3 The main object of this sequence of cuts is to ensure that the wood remains a square block for as long as possible so that as much waste removal as possible can be done safely with bandsaw or jigsaw cuts. ▼

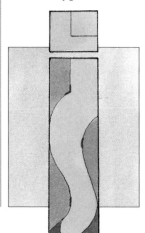

4 Cut the few remaining parts by hand with a coping saw. This removes the bulk of the waste. ▶

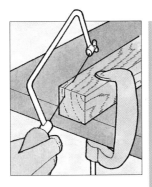

5 Begin the initial convex shaping with a spokeshave. Cut with the grain on a push stroke and rotate the work in the vice to ensure you are always cutting more or less horizontally and with the grain. Where outside curves are too tight for a spokeshave, use a chisel. ▶

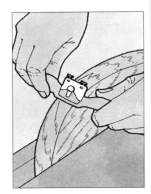

6 Use a convex-soled spokeshave to smooth inner, concave curves. Make sure the cut is always with the grain. Where curves are too tight for the spokeshave, use a gouge. ▶

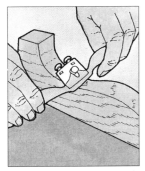

7 For even finer shaping use rasps, the woodworker's equivalent of files. Rifflers are small double-ended rasps. Their intricately curved ends mean they can smooth wood in awkward corners where no other tool can reach. ▼

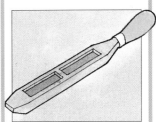

8 To summarize, work down through different kinds of abrading and shaping tools, from saws to spokeshaves, gouges, and rasps until you have a smooth enough finish to move on to sandpaper, working down through the grits. Make different profile sanding blocks from dowels, battens, and pieces of scrap wood to suit the shape of the work. ▼

OTHER SHAPING TOOLS

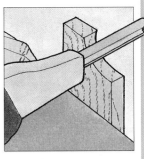

A Surform file is coarse and removes material quickly. It is often too coarse for woodwork, but can be very useful for shaping models or mockups made from materials other than wood. ▲

The drawknife is a very ancient woodworking tool used for fast shaping of components before they are more finely finished by a spokeshave. The blade is beveled on one side, and the tool cuts on a pull stroke in the direction of the grain. Hold the drawknife bevel upward to work a convex shape; hold bevel downward for a concave shape. ▲

The finger file is a narrow-belt power sander. It removes wood very fast and is best for the earlier stages of shaping. ▼

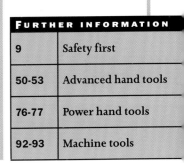

A flexible drive attached to a power drill can hold a range of small rotary rasps and burrs. These can reach into very tight curves. ▼

FURTHER INFORMATION	
9	Safety first
50-53	Advanced hand tools
76-77	Power hand tools
92-93	Machine tools

Bending and Laminating

It is not always possible to produce shaped components by cutting shapes from solid timber because short grain can make a component prone to failure.

Bending and laminating in a home workshop are generally confined to making a shape in one plane. It is possible to make steam bends in several planes, and it is possible to make panels with double curvature, but this needs quite advanced industrial machinery.

There are, however, several ways to create simple one-plane shapes.

BRICK OR STACK LAMINATING

This is a traditional method often seen in serpentine-shaped rails or bowed drawer fronts. The curved stack once completed is often veneered.

The method is rather like building a brick wall with shaped blocks of wood which are glued together. It is essential to make a full-size drawing of the shape you want to form. From this you

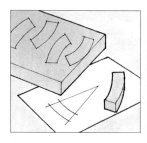

can decide on the best positioning of the brick courses to achieve a strong structure. ▲

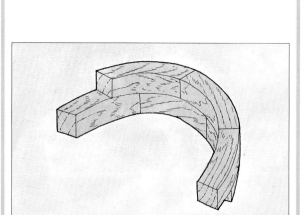

1 Make a cardboard pattern for the bricks. Build the shape, adding one layer at a time and allowing the glue to cure between layers. ▲

2 Smooth the surface with planes and spokeshaves when the required height has been reached. ▶

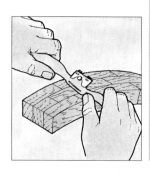

SAW KERFING

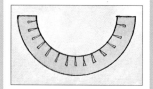

This is a method of bending a flat sheet of either solid wood or manmade board. The principle is based on the removal of a series of saw cuts or kerfs to a depth through the wood where the remaining material is capable of bending. Bending the material brings the tips of the saw kerfs together. ▲

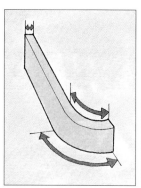

1 This method needs very careful calculation and a full-size drawing. You must ensure that you know the precise width of the saw kerf and calculate the distance between kerfs to give the required bend. ▲

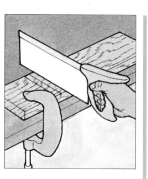

2 To calculate the spacing of the kerfs, mark the point at which the bending will start and saw a kerf here, leaving at least (⅛in). Measure and mark the radius of the curve from this first kerf. ▲

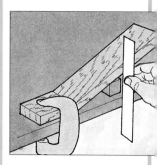

3 Clamp one end of the wood firmly, then lift the free end until the kerf closes. Wedge the free end in position at this point, and measure the distance between the bench and the underside of the board. This is the distance between kerfs. ▲

4 Sawing the kerfs with a radial arm saw is accurate but creates a fairly wide kerf unless you use a thin blade. Mark the distance between kerfs in pencil on the guide fence. ▶

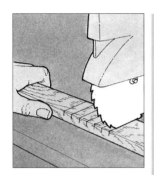

5 Other methods of sawing kerfs require a batten clamped to the work as a guide. Hand sawing is very labour intensive. A power circular saw requires a thin blade if you are not to cut wide kerfs. ▶

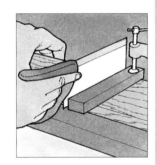

6 You will need formers around which to make the bend. By its very nature this method is not very strong since only the tips of the kerfs are glued. The cavities between them need a gap-filling glue or filler. The bend can be strengthened by applying thin ply to the kerfed face. ▶

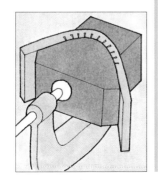

BENDING SOLID TIMBER

This traditional technique was used by the woodworkers, called "bodgers" who made Windsor chairs in the beech forests around High Wycombe.

The basic principle is that wood bends more easily when it is wet, i.e. before being seasoned, so if it is steamed it becomes supple once again.

The technique is possible in the home workshop but it needs a lot of work in the preparation of steaming equipment and bending jigs.

Steaming wood involves a lot of trial and error, it is more of an art than a science. Look on it as a way of learning and experimenting rather than just bending wood.

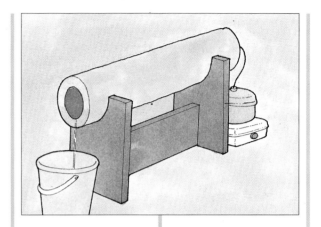

1 Make a simple steaming chamber from a large pipe or tube, which may be of plastic, metal or ceramic, and which can be insulated on the outside. Make bungs to fit both ends. Drill one bung to accept a rubber pipe from the steam generator. Drill the other bung to allow condensed water to escape; the tube therefore needs to be at a slight angle. ▲

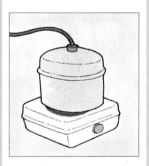

2 Find a suitable steam generator, for instance a large metal drum or a pressure cooker and solder a fitting so that the rubber pipe can be attached. Place the steam generator on a heat source. ▲

FURTHER INFORMATION	
9	Safety first
134-135	Veneers

3 Stack the wood to be bent in the tube, separating it with spacers to allow the steam to pass completely around it. The wood needs one hour of steaming for each inch of thickness. ▶

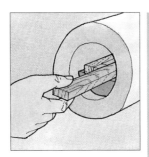

5 The outside form is composed of a flexible metal strap with handles. Fit the wooden handles and hardwood end stops using bolts. Make the distance between the end stops the same as the length of the wood being bent. ▶

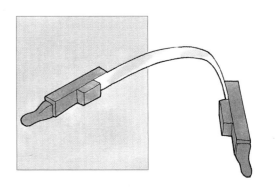

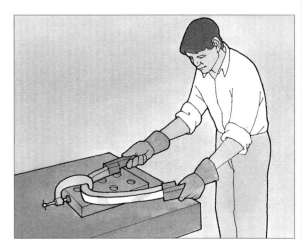

Outside bending form

Inside bending form

6 When the wood has been steamed, act quickly. You may need thick gloves to prevent scalding. Place the steamed component in the metal strap and bend it around the inside form. ▶

4 Inside and outside bending forms are needed. Make the inside form of particle board or MDF. It must be strong enough to withstand the clamping pressure while the wood dries, and it must offer some places where clamps can be located within the curve. ▲

7 Clamp and then leave the wood for several days to dry out. If you wish to remove and re-use the mold, you can do so after a day and leave the piece to dry naturally, as long as you make a tie across the two free ends to stop the bend from springing back. ▶

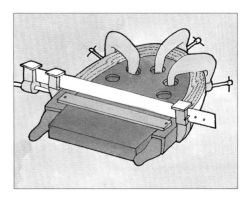

LAMINATING

Wood cut into thin strips is glued and pressed into shape between male and female forms.

Special thick veneers usually made from poplar are often used for the laminate. The grain follows a longitudinal direction in all the pieces, rather than being set at alternate right angles like plywood.

You can make your own veneers from solid wood, but this method is quite wasteful since the thickness of the saw means you waste as much as you use. Be very careful in following all safety procedures if you do cut your own strips. You will also need a thickness planer to smooth the laminate strips.

Laminating is not difficult, but it is essential to draw the full-size shape accurately; and when producing laminates with several curves, careful planning for clamping procedures is necessary as forms must sometimes be made in more than two parts to accommodate the curves.

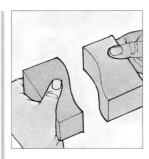

1 Make forms from manmade board such as particle board or MDF. Mark out the shape carefully, allowing for the thickness of the laminates. Make sure the shapes are precise and finish the internal faces of the forms exactly. ▲

2 Make the mold and the laminates wider than the laminated component to allow for cleaning up. Cut the laminates along the grain using a knife and straightedge. A decorative facing veneer may also be included in the laminate. ▲

3 Always make a trial run, bending and clamping the laminates without glue, to check the position of clamps and ensure that everything comes together tightly. ▼

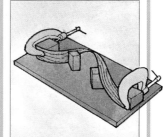

4 Use synthetic glue, preferably urea formaldehyde. Wrap the laminates in waxed paper to prevent the package from sticking to the forms. Place it in the forms, tighten the clamps, working from the center out, and leave to cure. To finish, trim the face edge, gauge and plane to width. ▼

FREE-FORM LAMINATING

The principle is similar to laminating, but no mold is used.

Bend the shape you want using only a single piece of laminate to begin with. Construct a series of clamping posts to hold the required shape.

When you are sure you can clamp in the required position, mark the position of the laminate in pencil on the posts.

Make the pack of glued laminates (strips of rubber bicycle inner tube are useful to bind the pack) and then clamp the laminates in position on the support posts. ▼

PRE-FORMING

Instead of laminating strips, pre-forming involves laminating sheets. Sometimes some of the veneer layers may be turned at 90 degrees to the main direction of grain, like plywood, to give more strength across the pre-form.

This method is mainly used in mass production. It is possible to undertake in the home workshop, but it is only really worthwhile making all the necessary jigs if several identical components are needed.

Easy Chair

The ergonomics of an easy chair, the way it relates to the human body, are more complex than for an upright chair. The complexity involved in designing a successful easy chair provides a real challenge, and a wide variety of approaches have been adopted by furniture designers.

The development of chair design in the 20th century vividly demonstrates a relationship with progress in other areas, such as architecture, as well as furniture design. Some of this development is due to the development of new materials, including metals and plastics, as well as techniques such as preform and laminating.

Even using natural wood and traditional techniques, the possibilities seem endless. While some chairs seem appropriate just for a time and soon look dated, others have become classic.

PRINCIPLES OF SEATING FOR RELAXATION

The back can be at almost any angle from almost upright to almost prone. Remember that, for comfort, the head needs support, so if the back slopes too far, it must be extended to support the head; otherwise, neck muscles begin to ache.

The height of the seat at the front can fall within a wide range from low to high. Remember a low seat is more difficult for elderly and infirm people to get out of.

If you are designing a lounge chair, which supports the lower legs and feet, remember you still have to get in and out.

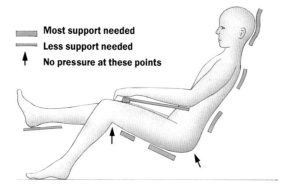

Most support needed
Less support needed
No pressure at these points

ALVAR AALTO • *Paimio chair* Still a chair that looks very much of today, it is the result of the convergence of a great designer and technological development. Much of Aalto's furniture features the use of laminated and preformed shapes. This is one of the first chairs to use the natural flex of the preformed seat and back to give comfort without the use of soft upholstery. ▲

Relationship between seat rake and depth If a seat is flat, it needs to be deep and soft to prevent the person from slipping out. ▶

A seat with a deep rake can be short, since the body is held in position and needs the minimum of soft upholstery for support. ▶

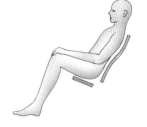

The softness of the seat cushions create a rake as they are deformed by body weight. ▶

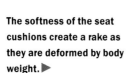

An approximate formula for seat rake to depth would be:
Where R=0 (level),
D=24 inches
Where R=5 inches
D=20 inches ▶

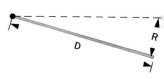

JUDITH AMES • *Reflection rocker*

A recent piece, but a timeless variation on the theme of rocking chairs. The color of the wood and the shaping of all the structural members give great elegance, complemented and enhanced by the back rails and the curve and length of the rockers. ▼

MARCEL BREUER • *Isokon long chair*

Breuer produced many innovative designs, first as a student than as a member of staff at the Bauhaus Design School in Germany during the 1920s and 1930s. When forced to leave Germany he first went to Britain and produced memorable designs, including this one for a laminated *chaise-longue*, before settling in America. ◄

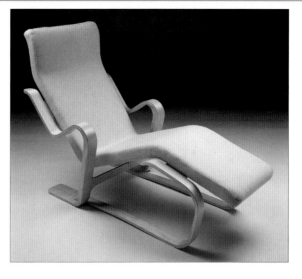

CHARLES EAMES • *670*

Lounge chair and ottoman
This chair is truly a classic piece of design; it is so much of its age, but sits well in interiors of all ages and styles. The combination of aluminum supports, rosewood veneered preforms, black leather and down fillings, combine to give great comfort as well as supreme elegance. One of the masterpieces of 20th century chair design. ▶

Chair sizes

The optimum measurements given here are suitable for adults of average height and build. ▶

h=10 to 16 inches
18 inches for elderly or infirm people.
d=24 to 20 inches
r=6 inches
Col (Center of lumbar) =8 inches
sh=20 inches
n=22 inches
h=8 inches
ad=12 inches
ah=4 inches

ar=2 inches
l=22 inches
w=18 to 24 inches
wba=20 inches minimum

FURTHER INFORMATION	
108-109	Chairs and their construction
152-163	Module 8: easy chair

Index

Credits

Quarto would like to thank all the furniture makers who have kindly allowed us to include their work in this book.

We would also like to thank the following for their permission to reproduce copyright material: p. 31 *Good Woodworking* magazine; p. 90 & 91 (Robert Venturi) Knoll International; p. 120 & 121 (Hans Wegner) PP Mobler APS, Denmark; p. 151 (Andrew Whateley) photo by Frank Thurston; p. 170 (Alvar Aalto) Artek, Helsinki; p. 171 (Charles Eames) manufactured by Vitra Ltd, London; (Marcel Breuer) manufactured by Windmill Furniture, London.

In addition, Quarto would like to give a special thanks to Axminster Power Tool Centre, Chard Street, Axminster, Devon, who very kindly lent the tools and equipment featured in this book.

AUTHOR'S ACKNOWLEDGEMENTS

In writing this book I am aware of specific thanks needed, but also a sense of general support from the many woodworkers I have known. Specifically, thanks to my wife Raye and to Quarto's staff for their help and encouragement. Generally, however, having been concerned with the woodworking and furniture trade for over 30 years, and also been involved in craft and design education, I remember my many colleagues and friends. The world of furniture craftsmen is full of interesting and lively people who gain pleasure from designing and making fine pieces that in themselves give pleasure to the recipients. I recognize and thank them for their influences. I have taught in many education institutions and I must thank my many colleagues for their interest and support. I have been fortunate to have known many students in furniture making and design studies, and have gained much enjoyment from seeing them develop and then utilize their skills, especially those from Rycotewood College and the School of Architecture at Oxford Brookes University. In particular, I would like to thank the staff and students of the Furniture College at Letterfrack, Co. Galway, in the Connemara area of Ireland, and especially graduate Joel Friel who helped make the prototypes.